T0278298

YOUR J
FINAN
FREED

YOUR JOURNEY TO
FINANCIAL
FREEDOM

A Step-by-Step
Guide to
Achieving Wealth
and Happiness

JAMILA SOUFFRANT

HANOVER
SQUARE
PRESS

HANOVER
SQUARE
PRESS™

ISBN-13: 978-1-335-00779-7

Your Journey to Financial Freedom

Hanover Square Press
22 Adelaide St. West, 41st Floor
Toronto, Ontario M5H 4E3, Canada
HanoverSqPress.com
BookClubbish.com

Printed in U.S.A.

To Zach, Luke and Blake. I wouldn't have had the guts to follow my dreams if it weren't for you. I'm so lucky to be your mom.

To my husband, Woody, thank you for being a true partner and friend. I love the life we've created together.

To my mom, Debby, everything I am is because of your sacrifice and love. I'll always be your baby girl.

To you, my dear reader, who will now become a Journeyer on this path with me. I hope this book helps you make your wildest dreams come true.

YOUR JOURNEY TO
FINANCIAL
FREEDOM

TABLE OF CONTENTS

INTRODUCTION

When I was only eight months old, my mother faced a difficult decision that would affect both our lives forever. Her father had filed a visa application on her behalf to move to the United States, which finally got approved. The issue was that the visa application was submitted before my birth, so there was no accompanying paperwork for me to join her. This left my mother with a dilemma: to leave me behind in Jamaica and pursue better opportunities in the US or to stay in Jamaica with me. As a twenty-year-old single mom, she made the brave choice to go to a country she'd never visited before with no money, just a piece of paper with an address and phone number of someone to contact when she arrived. My mom's story is not unlike those of many immigrants who come to the US and take enormous risks by leaving everything they know behind to have a chance at creating a better life for themselves and their family.

Despite the challenges of being in a new country and hardly knowing anyone but a few family members, my mom did her best to acclimate and got her first job through a cousin at a local Kentucky Fried Chicken. Eventually, nine months later, my grandmother's and my paperwork were approved and we were able to join her in New York City. I was just under two years old when we were finally reunited. As a mother now, I know how difficult that must have been for her to make that choice to leave me behind at such a young age to venture into the unknown without a guarantee of what would come next. But I also know that the hope she had for a better life for me outweighed the fear of doing something risky.

My mother's upbringing was not one that allowed her to explore her own potential or independence. She grew up in poverty, with no running water for most of her childhood and only the necessities. She recounts vivid memories of the many times she went to school hungry. After having me, she vowed to herself to improve our lives and find a different path. Despite limited resources and no internet to easily search for information, she persevered and sought out any available help in this new country. She utilized the yellow pages to locate resources and was determined to advance her situation. She received government aid to supplement her income, but knew she'd have to further her education to increase her earning potential, so she pursued her associate's degree, followed by a bachelor's, and years later, a master's degree. Since she was a single mother who couldn't always afford childcare, I became her constant companion, earning me the nickname "Pocket-book." She recalls the many times she had to take me with her to classes and appointments in the rain and freezing winters, weather she was not used to growing up on a tropical island. When she did her homework, she gave me a paper and crayon so that I could get my "homework" done too. Although I may not remember all the specifics due to my young age at that time, her unwavering drive and determination left a lasting imprint on my psyche and played a significant role in shaping who I am today. I may not have been born into money, but I had something more valuable, a loving mother who believed in me and showed me that anything was possible.

This I hope gives some insight into why I felt inspired to pursue financial independence, and why I am going to ask you to do what others will tell you is impossible or unrealistic.

When I started working full-time in my early twenties, I said that I would never work for anyone after the age of thirty. I had such an ambitious can-do attitude. I didn't like the constraints of my corporate America job and didn't want to have to call anyone else boss. I would sit at my cubicle crafting ways in which quitting at thirty was possible. I thought I could do it by investing in real estate and starting my own business. By then, I already had one property in my portfolio, a studio apartment in an up-and-coming area of Brooklyn. I was also working on an online magazine, *Empress*, that I had created in college with my best friend. My hope was that the magazine would take off and provide a full source of income. But somewhere along the way, as I approached my late twenties, I realized my dream of quitting the mainstream workforce was not going to happen. By then, my zeal for thinking outside of the box had slowed. I no longer had the energy needed to put into the online magazine to make it a true success. My friend and I decided to call it quits on the magazine. Every other entrepreneurial venture I tried, I either quit or watched fail before I could see any real progress.

As I got older, I began to accept that my big dreams of becoming my own boss and a millionaire would not come true. At twenty-nine, I'd gotten married to my college sweetheart, Woody, and we began making plans to start a family. My ambitious goal of avoiding the never-ending cycle of the daily grind faded away, and I instead resigned myself to following the path of so many others by settling for a steady job until retirement. In doing so, I found myself becoming exactly the type of person I had once promised myself I would never be. Someone who lived solely to work, spending the majority of their day being governed by others, and exchanging their time for a paycheck.

I had a few nudges that would occasionally wake me up from what I felt like was me sleepwalking through life. A pivotal one came at thirty-one in 2014, when I found myself stuck in a four-hour commute home from hell, seven months pregnant with my first child, Zach. My typical commute took about an hour and a half each way, but on this particular day, the traffic gods were not pleased. Everything that could go wrong did, turning my already tough commute into a nightmare. Overwhelmed by frustration, I broke down and cried in my car, and then again when I finally arrived home to my husband.

I didn't want this to be my life forever; this couldn't be my life forever. The next day at work, I googled *how to quit my job* and *how to retire early*. A few podcasts and blogs came up and it was then that I was initially introduced to the Financial Independence Retire Early (FIRE) movement. I slowly started to read blogs at work and listen to podcasts on my commute about everyday people building wealth through working a regular nine-to-five. There were no fancy methods or complicated strategies, they were just spending less than they earned and investing aggressively to reach a level in which they could quit their jobs and retire early. A seed was instantly planted. I had finally found a viable, proven pathway to freedom from life in a cubicle. Woody and I started making changes to our finances like trading our expensive luxury cars for more economical cars, budgeting, and investing more. Fast-forward to 2016. We were making progress with our finances, but when I found out that I was pregnant with my second child, Luke, I knew that it was time to get even more intentional and serious about our Financial Independence (FI) journey. Sure, I'd "missed" my goal of not working for anyone after thirty, but it wasn't too late to turn my life around. It's never too late to turn it around. I found a renewed sense of purpose and drive being pregnant with Luke. Although my children motivated me to take more courageous strides, I knew that this pursuit was something that I had to do for myself too. I didn't want to spend the majority of my time doing a job that didn't bring me joy or stuck in traffic. Just as my mom set that example for me on what it meant to go for it and chart a new path different from the one she was expected to travel, I wanted to be that example for my kids too. I desired to teach them that they could accomplish anything they set their minds to and that they need not conform to society's notion of happiness. I wished for them to design and live life on their own terms. I felt that it was my responsibility to lead a life that I could be proud of, to demonstrate to them that it could be achieved, and most importantly, to prove to myself that it was attainable. The pathway to the freedom that I wanted and the ability to do what I wanted with my time and energy was going to be through taking control of my finances.

I decided to officially start *Journey to Launch*, originally called *MrsBudgetFab*, as a blog in 2016, to chronicle my journey to FI. At thirty-three years old I declared my seven-year plan to reach Financial Independence and quit my corporate job goal by forty years old. An excerpt from my very first post on February 19, 2016, read:

> *There has been a fire smoldering inside of me, wanting to burn free and wild. I will not suppress it any longer. Maybe my story and journey will help others like me who feel somewhat confused on this journey of life. Primarily, I am here to learn and boy do I have a lot of learning to do. I also know that I can make an impact on the world with my story and that's where we start on this path together.*

I soon changed the name of my blog from *MrsBudgetFab* to *Journey to Launch* as I quickly realized that budgeting was a key but small part of what it took to ultimately reach FI. The name *Journey to Launch* encompassed more of what the path to FI actually looks like, as it takes into account not just the end goal of FI but the exciting journey that it takes to reach that ultimate goal. It also demonstrated the idea of aspiring to something bigger than what you currently have. I wanted to share my journey and help readers on their own journey to launch to financial freedom and FI.

I started the podcast, *Journey to Launch*, a year later. I also got pregnant again with my third child, Blake. As you can probably tell, each child inspired and pushed me further on my path. Getting pregnant with Blake was no different and caused me to make my boldest, riskiest moves yet. By then, I was thirty-five years old and balancing my demanding corporate job and commute with *Journey to Launch* on the side. I had progressed significantly in what I refer to as the Aviator phase, which is the third of the five stages of the Journeyer process required to achieve FI (something you'll learn about in Chapter 2 of this book). Once my husband and I had saved and invested a significant portion of our earnings into our investment accounts, I made the decision to move on to the fourth stage of the Journeyer process and attain work flexibility by leaving my day job. I had the liberty to resign from my position and establish my own business on my own terms. Although I had not yet achieved complete financial independence, I had attained most of its benefits. That's what I want for you too, and with this book I hope to help guide you on a path to achieving it.

If you've read an article online you have probably seen a highlighted word or phrase, known as a hyperlink. You're interested in the story but know a hyperlink would give you even more information. Sometimes you ignore a hyperlink, but sometimes you click, going deeper and deeper down the rabbit hole. Our life is like one big story and as we write it we come across hyperlinks too. It can happen when you overhear something interesting like a person talking about a place they visited or a show they watched and you want to learn more about it. Maybe you end up visiting that place or pick up a book on the subject to learn more. Sometimes the hyperlinks don't mean much, but sometimes they can change your world as you know it. Your curiosity could lead to starting a new job or meeting someone who becomes a mentor. Maybe you discover a whole new way of life. For me, it all started when I looked up the words *how to quit my job* and found an article that mentioned the "FIRE movement"—something I had never heard of before. That moment changed the course of my life. It didn't happen right away and it took me many more hyperlinks to get to where I am now. But you picking up this book is like you clicking on a new hyperlink in your life. The hyperlinks I've clicked on by first discovering FIRE and being intrigued by it allowed me to quit my corporate job.

In the following chapters, I will be sharing some recommended percentages and formulas to help you navigate your path, but you don't have to create a rigid plan around them. They are only meant to be reference points to help you get started or for when you need guidance. You don't have to live by formulas and percentages. You don't have to count every penny and live on a restricted budget forever.

These formulas and percentages are merely meant to be a guideline, like the bumper guards that bowling alleys give kids and less talented bowlers like myself that guarantee no matter how bad we throw, the ball doesn't go into the gutter. I want you to build your own guardrails and safety nets that allow you to be free with money.

Now, I don't use a budget day to day, some months I don't even look. Why do I feel comfortable managing my finances this way? It's because I've found the balance between my current lifestyle goals and long-term financial goals. I'm able to pay off credit card debt every month. My family is on track for our FI goals. I'm okay with my investments.

Could things be more optimized to save and invest more money? Sure. But that's not the main priority for me right now. Instead, I'm leaning more into spending and enjoying the right now. Don't get me wrong, I still have moments of fear and question *are we really good?* When I have those feelings, I look at the plan I've created to give me assurance that I'm still on the right path. It's that sense of security in the now and the future that I want you to enjoy after reading this book.

You don't have to become a personal finance expert or be good with math to be successful on your FI journey. I'm still learning and making mistakes just like anyone else. My ability to make it as far as I have is not because of pure skill but a mixture of luck (something you can't control) and a lot of perseverance (something you can control). Best of all, I'm really just like you because I'm still on this journey, maybe a few steps ahead but still willing to learn and adapt as I continue on my path too.

To assist you in achieving FI, this book has been organized into four parts. In Part 1, where we focus on awareness, we explore the what, why, and how of FI. This lays the foundation for your journey and explains the five Journeyer stages you must work through to reach FI; the six components that make up part of the FI formula; and how all the components work together to help you reach your financial and life goals. In Part 2, where we focus on gathering information and making the journey enjoyable, I introduce you to the Guacamole lifestyle levels to help you figure out the quality of lifestyle you want to live, as well as help you identify your starting point and your desired FI end point. You will discover where you are on your journey relative to your ultimate FI goal and learn how to craft a plan to reach FI by aligning your life and financial objectives. In Part 3, where we shift focus towards taking action, I provide guidance on how to execute your plan to reach FI by improving your mindset and habits, increasing your income, optimizing expenses, paying off debt, and investing. Finally, in Part 4, where we hone in on making your plan sustainable and enjoyable, we explore ways to stay the course on your journey toward FI.

As you embark on your FI journey, it's important to remember that your plan is not set in stone. The process of planning and executing is a continuous loop, and adjustments may need to be made along the way. Part 2 will help you identify your starting and end points, but you may need to revisit them as you progress through the other parts. Part 3 is all about taking action and implementing your plan, but you may find that your initial plan needs to be adjusted based on what works best for you. You may find that in order to make your journey to financial independence more sustainable, you need to adjust your lifestyle or financial goals. As an example, when I initially created my FI plan in 2016, I set a goal of achieving FI in seven years by aggressively saving and investing while working in corporate America. During the first two years of implementing my plan, my husband and I were able to save and invest $169,000. However, I soon realized that this plan was unsustainable due to the demands of my commute, growing family, and side business. After some reflection, I recognized that there were other pathways available to me. I had the opportunity to quit my job and pursue entrepreneurship full-time which could either delay or accelerate my FI goal depending on the success of my business. Moreover, I came to the realization that my target lifestyle needed to be more realistic and authentic to my preferences. I revised my plan by adjusting my end goal and changing my journey to one that aligned with my desired lifestyle. While this meant that I may possibly reach my FI goal at a later age, perhaps at fifty-five, I was content with this as long as I could enjoy more freedom and flexibility along the way.

As you go on this journey, there will be people who doubt you, who tell you that it can't be done. They may say the lifestyle and freedom you are looking to achieve is only for a certain group of people. You may even think to yourself that you're not smart enough, talented enough, too old, or too young to get started. However, despite any such doubts, you have ample time and are just as capable to realize the dreams you have for yourself. There's a popular Zen saying, "When the student is ready, the teacher will appear." That's one reason why you have picked up this book at this moment.

I don't know what it's like to never have to work for money ever again. I'm still on my journey to launch, but what I can say from my experience is that you will unlock more flexibility and freedom with your money and your life at every stage of the journey. And that's true even if you're not technically financially independent. *Yet*.

I have gained a wealth of knowledge through my personal experiences and conducting hundreds of interviews for the *Journey to Launch* podcast, in which I interviewed experts and individuals who are on their own journey toward achieving FI. I have distilled this information, along with my own experiences, into frameworks and steps that you can follow. These guidelines will help you avoid making common mistakes and achieve success along the way. In this book, I want to equip you with the necessary tools to design your own unique, enjoyable journey. My mom may have had few material resources, but she had something even more valuable: inner courage to dare to try, which is what I'm asking you to do now too: have the courage to try. Wherever you are now in your life and regardless of where you are starting off financially, you can have a life of more freedom, options, and happiness.

PART 1:

THE WHAT, WHY, AND
HOW OF FINANCIAL INDEPENDENCE

1

FINANCIAL INDEPENDENCE IS WITHIN YOUR REACH

Imagine it's your first day at FLY Finance High. Like any school, groups are sitting together at tables based on special interests—athletics, music, robotics club, etc. In this school, there are several tables with finance/money groups. It's noisy, chaotic, and you're trying to find a place to sit so you're scoping out which of the groups you should join. Each table has someone encouraging you to sit with them as you walk by. One table is the "Basic Personal Finance" group and they are all about maintaining the status quo when it comes to dealing with money—budget so you can pay down your debt and take vacations, improve your credit score, and invest the standard 10–15% of your income. If you choose to sit with them, you'll do okay. Follow their rules and you'll be able to buy a house and car, take vacations, and pay down debt, eventually. Sounds like the perfect group to sit with until you realize that the result of a standard financial plan is that you'll also have to work until the standard retirement age (between sixty-five and sixty-seven years old), if you're lucky. This group keeps you locked into the work and spend cycle. The dreams that you secretly buried deep within won't die quickly but rather by a million paper cuts. At the end of your life, you'll look back and wonder how much time you wasted by just doing enough and following the status quo with your life and finances.

Then you look across the room and see another group, the "Elite FIRE" table. At first they come off a bit intense and numbers focused. Their advice is that you need to invest at least 50% of your income (more if you can), become super frugal, and give up your attachment to material things and expensive items. It's all about optimizing and maximizing your numbers so that you can reach your financial goals as quickly as possible and retire way earlier than the standard age. The trade-off to achieve this accelerated path to freedom means you may have to set your lifestyle standards to below what you actually desire, forever. To this group, spending as little as possible is the goal and worth any absence of luxury or comfort if it means you don't have to work again.

You love the sound of this because it feels like the ultimate freedom: quitting the job you hate and retiring early. Then you'd have more time to do the things you enjoy, like spending time with family and friends, traveling, or exploring your hobbies. As you begin cutting back, you realize this life is just not sustainable. Sure, you can see living frugally for a couple years but forever?! You just can't imagine it. At the end of your life, you might look back and wonder how much you missed and regret all the things you couldn't indulge in because of these strict limitations.

There are other tables in the cafeteria too—the "YOLO" table which is all about living your best life today, future be damned. There's the "Get Rich Quick" table where they are always coming up with a way to earn faster—expenses and their financial future are not a concern because they can always earn back what they spend.

Each table offers a different way of handling your money, and with it a different path in life.

While my characterization of the Basic Personal Finance and the Elite FIRE tables are generalizations, that's a good overview of how each group talks about money and the trade-offs you'll have to make when following their rules. Within personal finance, you'll often run into these two broad camps. When I first became intentional about my finances it was like walking into this imaginary FLY Finance High, I knew the Basic Personal Finance table wasn't for me because I didn't want to work forever, whether I enjoyed the job or not. For a while, I tried to hang out at the Elite FIRE table but realized I didn't want my life to be dictated by a strict budget. I saw a middle ground and decided to create my own table with my own rules, picking and choosing which advice worked for me depending on which season of life I was in.

Dear Journeyer, I invite you to join me at this table.

Joining me means you won't ever have to feel stuck or without options. You don't need to be super frugal or talk about money all day to reach your goals. You can spend lavishly on things that matter and yes, sometimes even spend recklessly (within reason of course) without jeopardizing your financial security or future. You'll still have the option to quit your job, leave a situation, take a break from traditional work, or just flat out retire earlier than the standard age.

The best part is that you can enjoy your life right from where you are today, while you embark on your journey.

A brief history of FIRE

I discovered FIRE around 2014 but the movement has been around for decades. One of the earliest books to talk about the concept of financial independence was *Your Money or Your Life, Transforming Your Relationship with Money and Achieving Financial Independence* by Joe Dominguez and Vicki Robin. Originally published in 1992, *Your Money or Your Life* talked about the concepts of breaking free of the cycle of work and making money just to pay off debt and bills so that you could take back control of your life. The message was well received enough that the book made the *New York Times* Best Seller list and author Vicki Robin appeared on the *Oprah Winfrey Show* twice, in 1992 and 1995, to talk about this idea of conscious spending and separating your work from your life. Over thirty years later, the message is still relevant.

The FIRE movement reemerged in the mainstream thanks to the internet and popular blogs like *Mr. Money Mustache* and podcasters who began sharing their own experience. I remember when I first found the podcast *Mad Fientist*. The host, Brandon, interviewed various people who were pursuing FIRE, ranging from teachers to engineers. They shared stories of how they were saving and investing their money in the pursuit of quitting their job or how they had actually accomplished FI and were now living life on their own terms, traveling the world and controlling their time.

When I heard stories of what seemed to be average people with normal jobs being able to exit the traditional nine-to-five, I knew I had found a potential pathway to freedom for myself. The instructions seemed clear: get rid of debt, spend a lot less than you make, live frugally, and put as much as you can in your investment accounts and you could be free from working for anyone else in ten years or less.

FINANCIAL INDEPENDENCE VS. FINANCIAL FREEDOM

Since the terms *financial independence* and *financial freedom* often are used interchangeably and can mean different things to different people, I want to define how I will be using them in this book.

Financial freedom for one person can mean they feel good about their ability to pay their bills on time and for another person it can mean they feel secure in having money in their savings account to cover emergencies. I define *financial freedom* as the ability to have options and control over how you handle your money. So being able to pay your bills even if you have debt or having money saved for an emergency even if you don't have millions in the bank means you have achieved some level of financial freedom.

Similarly, one person may say *financial independence* and mean that they don't have to depend on anyone else for money as in "I'm financially independent from my parents." When I use the term *financially independent* I mean being independent from anyone and everything, including a job. This means the money you've accumulated in your investment accounts can cover your expenses indefinitely. Think trust fund baby who was born into money and doesn't ever need to work, thanks to Great-grandpa Joe's entrepreneurial success. But in your case, you created the trust fund for yourself.

> **Financial Independence (FI)** is when you reach a level where the income generated from your investments and assets can pay for your lifestyle expenses without your needing to work. You can still choose to work and bring in money, but if you decided not to ever work again, you'd be okay financially. The key point here is that working is a choice.
>
> **Financial Freedom** means your ability to have options and security with your money. You can experience financial freedom without being financially independent.

We all have varying levels of how much we'd want to have to feel financially free or financially independent. One person may say they are financially independent once they've reached $1,000,000 invested and another person may feel that they'd need $3,000,000 to feel financially independent. One person's financial independence is another person's Financially Okay.

You've reached financial independence when the amount in your investment portfolios (which includes both principal and interest) and the income it generates covers all of your expenses. Your investment portfolio includes retirement accounts like 401(k), 403(b), Roth IRA, Traditional IRA, non-retirement taxable accounts such as regular brokerage accounts, and assets like income-generating properties, or cash in a bank account.

If it seems impossible now, why should you even try?

You might be thinking, *But Jamila, I wasn't born into money.*

I have a lot of debt. I feel like I'm starting too late. This goal of having enough money to never have to work again seems impossible.

When I show you how to calculate your FI number in Chapter 8, the number may seem too big and too far away to even attempt to pursue. I get it. At first, my number felt impossible too. The fact that you have an idea of this number—and please remember it can change—means you have something to work toward. You know the saying, shoot for the moon and if you don't make it, you'll still land among the stars. The FI number is your Moonshot. It's the audacious end goal, but if you don't reach it in the desired time frame that you've set for yourself, you still will be in a better place than where you started or if you never had tried.

Let's say you calculated your number as $1.5 million and based on your current starting point you assess that you can reach that number in fifteen years. But fifteen years later instead of having $1.5 million you "only" have $1 million. But is having $1 million really a failure? You are among the stars and doing better than the 49% of adults ages fifty-five to sixty-six who had no personal retirement savings in 2017. This is why I think everyone should joyfully strive toward this goal, because even missing the mark puts you in a better place from where you will be if you don't start.

After binging on what felt like a million hours of podcasts and reading tons of blogs on the subject of financial independence, I began to tinker with our numbers on my own spreadsheet. I needed to understand how much Woody and I would need to become financially independent and wanted to see how much time it would take for us to get there.

When I first told Woody about my interest in the FIRE

movement, I could tell he was open to the idea of it but not convinced it was achievable. He, like me, grew up seeing the adults around him work whether they liked it or not until they couldn't work anymore. We also had no real-life examples of people who had retired successfully in the traditional way and now here I was talking about retiring early. But unlike him, I had immersed myself in a world where impossible things like retiring early, living off $30,000 a year and traveling the world were normal. Over the next couple of months, I continued to share interesting stories I heard with him. I was especially excited to share with him the stories I thought he could relate to like a teacher retiring with a million-dollar portfolio, because he is also a teacher.

Eventually after tinkering with my spreadsheet, I showed him what was actually possible for us. I had a column showing where our investments and numbers would be if we changed nothing about our financial habits as well as scenarios that showed how much more money we could have in the future if we adjusted our spending, saving, and investing habits. The difference was staggering. On one hand if we saved and invested the bare minimum as we had been doing, (at the time I was investing only up to my company match and my husband was only putting 2% toward his retirement account) we'd barely be able to retire comfortably at the standard retirement age. However, if we made some changes we would definitely be able to retire comfortably at the standard retirement age and if we decided to become even more aggressive with our investing habits, we'd be able to hit our FI number and retire early well before the standard retirement age.

EVERYONE SHOULD PURSUE FI

The real benefit of pursuing FI is not in the accumulation of assets and the growth of your accounts, but rather it's what you gain and who you become *while* you are on the pursuit. While you are on your way to FI you have to learn to enjoy and revel in the skills, confidence, and resilience that transform you more than any number can. The money and economic gains will enhance your journey but all that can and may come and go. Your accounts may fluctuate with changes in interest rates, news events, and other things outside of your control, but who you become can't be diminished or taken from you. *That is real power and freedom.* By not solely focusing on the final outcome of accumulating wealth, but also taking into account the personal growth, knowledge, and emotions that come with the journey toward financial security, you can begin to find enjoyment and fulfillment in your life regardless of your current financial situation. As you work toward your goal, you'll discover many ways that achieving FI can positively impact your life:

- You'll gain more control over your life and can have more options about how you want to live and work.

- Achieving financial independence can provide greater security and stability, both for you and your family.

- Financial independence can allow you to pursue your passions and interests, rather than being tied to a job or career that may not be fulfilling.

- Financial independence can provide the freedom to travel or live in different places.

- The things you'll need to do to move through the various stages of financial independence will lead to a greater sense of accomplishment and personal satisfaction.

- Financial independence can provide peace of mind, knowing that you have the resources to handle emergencies or unexpected expenses.

QUESTIONS YOU MAY BE ASKING

What About the RE in FIRE?

The *RE* in *FIRE* stands for Retire Early. Oftentimes when people first hear of the FIRE movement, people can get with the first part, the FI, but the second part seems to mess them up. Some people can't imagine a world in which they don't work and see the act of retiring early as impossible, selfish, or unrealistic.

If we leave off the RE part and focus on the FI part, we really get to the idea that you are working toward having enough money to sustain your life. What you choose to do after you achieve FI is your business. Maybe you still work your corporate job because you love it. Maybe you start your own business or maybe you literally decide to lie down on a beach and drink mojitos every day.

You can either choose to indulge in the RE of the FIRE, like Purple, who was on episodes 126 and 289 of the podcast. She began her pursuit of FI back in 2015 when she was twenty-five years old and reached it at thirty years old. She was able to retire on a $500,000 investment portfolio and only spends about $20,000 a year in retirement. She doesn't actively work anymore and lives off her investment portfolio while still traveling the world and indulging in her idea of luxury. Her days are spent reading, running, and doing whatever she wants.

A lot of the people I've interviewed who have reached FI still continue to work and bring in income. Sometimes they are earning more money than when they were actively pursuing financial independence. They enjoy making money but can now choose *how* they earn it. The decision to retire after reaching financial independence is yours to make.

It doesn't matter whether you're starting this journey with the intention to quit your corporate job and start your own business, have more options with where and how you work, or retire early and chill all day. You can't help but level up and gain the skills and knowledge that will help you improve your ability to make money. Learning to create a budget that works for you, negotiating your salary, side hustling, investing, and everything else you learn along the way improve not only your financial capabilities but also your quality of life.

Do I Really Want to Retire Early or Do I Just Hate My Job?

If you really are honest with yourself about why you want to reach FIRE, you may discover, as I did, that it was more about leaving your current situation than not working ever again. Maybe your current work is not fulfilling, you're not making enough money, you have to sacrifice too much family time, dislike your coworkers and your manager, or maybe it's all of the above. Like me, you hate the idea of having to clock in or ask someone else for time off. Working is not what most people are trying to run away from. It's working in disre-spectful, oppressive environments that don't pay enough that most people want to escape. If this is your situation, it's even more crucial to be on this journey. Financial independence is worth pursuing because of the options you'll find along the way, which will help you enjoy life.

LeBron James and Oprah have more than enough money to never have to work again, but they still do. They are not showing up to check off boxes but are still competitive, cre-ative, and at the top of their fields, which challenges the idea that if you had enough money, you'd automatically want to stop working. If you find something you love, that you're good at, that challenges you and that even contributes to the world you may never want to stop working. In fact, you may find that something inside you pushes you to work harder.

Okay, Fine, But What if I Love My Job?

First of all, congratulations on finding work you love and enjoy—not many people find that. But even if you feel valued, are challenged, are compensated well, have amazing benefits, and a good work-life balance where you don't feel the need to sacrifice family time for your job, embarking on this jour-ney still benefits you. All of those circumstances may not stay the same forever and you may also change your mind about what makes you happy. What if five years down the line you decide that you want to start a family and take off as much time as possible to be home with your children or you decide that you want to take care of a sick family member? Maybe you develop a hobby and want to spend unrestricted time ex-ploring it more, feel tired and burned out and want to take a break without an expectation to have to go back to work. If and when that happens, you will be happy you started on the path because by then, you'll have given yourself enough runway to make a decision from a place of financial power and not dependency on working to pay the bills.

FINANCIAL FREEDOM AT EVERY STAGE OF THE JOURNEY

Unlike financial independence, financial freedom is not about having all the money you'd ever need and never having to work again. Financial freedom is more about the options you have and the joy it allows you to experience day to day. You don't need to have a million dollars in the bank or be completely debt-free to have financial freedom. For example, financial freedom can look like your ability to pay for childcare or go out to eat at your favorite restaurant without going into debt or feeling guilty that you should be doing something else with your money. You have the freedom and flexibility in how you earn and spend your money. Financial freedom is something you can experience on your way to financial independence.

I know this may challenge your ideas of what financial freedom means. You may be thinking to yourself, *I still can't pay for all the things I want in life and still have to work a job I hate. Tell me again how I'm financially free, Jamila?* Here's the thing: The levels of freedom depend on the lifestyle you want to live, and your lifestyle determines the financial thresholds you'll need to achieve. But regardless of your circumstances, *there is freedom at every level* because you have access to something that you otherwise wouldn't have had. For example, you can experience more financial freedom even if you still have debt, if you have figured out a way to manage your current debt and have a sustainable plan to pay it off without going into more debt. The sense of control you have will give you some peace of mind as opposed to not having a plan and not feeling like you have any control over your finances. Having financial hope and financial optimism is also a form of financial freedom.

In order to achieve complete financial independence but experience financial freedom along the way, you'll need to become financially fluid, allowing yourself to be flexible in how you deal with life as it happens.

2

THE JOURNEYER STAGES

Financial independence and even financial freedom can seem far away. But you'll be able to unlock more options, more joy, and more leverage with your money as you continue on your journey to launch. Honestly, that's the whole point of being on the journey in the first place. It's the twists and turns in the adventure that matter, because what I've heard about achieving complete financial independence is that the ultimate goal is usually experienced in one quiet moment. That elusive, seemingly mythical moment where you check your spreadsheets (twice) and realize you've surpassed the number you set for yourself way back when.

This journey will feel like a marathon and will take some time. Depending on when you find this book and where you are financially, the pursuit may even feel unfeasible. Just like training for a marathon, achieving financial independence involves breaking the journey into sections. Similar to finding ways to enjoy shorter training runs, it's important to find ways to enjoy the smaller financial sprints, so you can stay motivated and committed to achieving the larger goal. This could involve celebrating milestones along the way or finding satisfaction in the progress made toward financial independence.

This need for financial sprints is the reason I created the five Journeyer stages. I believe they encompass everything I've personally experienced so far as well as what I most often see in people who are pursuing or who have achieved financial independence. The amount of time it takes you to reach financial independence can take decades. Breaking the financial journey into shorter sprints can feel more manageable and less overwhelming. Each short sprint helps you build endurance and prepare for the bigger challenges ahead.

Since we all have different starting points, the stages provide an easy way to identify where you are now and the stages ahead. This chapter is meant to be a reference guide for you while you work through the book and advance through each of the stages. You'll find a basic overview of each stage that includes:

- a quick rundown of your financial situation,

- what you should be working on, and

- how to know when you can advance to the next stage.

I came up with the following names for the stages to keep with the theme of launching into space. I envisioned an astronaut preparing to go on their first mission, and as they get deeper into their training, they are able to move up in rank. The five stages are:

THE 5 JOURNEYER STAGES

1: THE EXPLORER STAGE

At the beginning of your journey you're exploring your surroundings, getting the lay of the land, and reviewing the mission. In this stage you learn the basics and do the groundwork that will help you throughout all other stages of your mission. It prepares you for the rigorous training ahead.

2: THE CADET STAGE

This is the start of your training, where your hands get dirty. This may also feel like the hardest part because it's the first time you've used your mind/body in this capacity. How much you need to "get in shape" depends on your starting point. Stick with it and get through this stage and you'll see why it was all worth it.

3: THE AVIATOR STAGE

You've gone through the toughest part of your training but there's still a lot to learn, including more advanced techniques.

4: THE COMMANDER STAGE

You've learned both the basic and advanced techniques and can apply them to the real world. You are no longer in training and can steer or take control of the rocket yourself.

5: THE CAPTAIN STAGE

You have not only the knowledge but also the experience to lead your own mission. You have full autonomy.

> Take the quiz over at
> www.yourjourneytofinancialfreedom.com
> to find your Journeyer stage

Now that you have a general overview of each Journeyer level, let's dive into the details of each stage.

 # EXPLORER STAGE

YOUR MAIN MISSION:
Become Financially Stable

Your Current Financial Situation:

- You may feel out of control and stressed out about your finances.
- You might be unable to pay your bills or be racking up debt month after month.
- Your current expenses may be more than your current income.

What You Should Be Working On:

- Organizing your finances and understanding what your bills and liabilities are in comparison to what you're earning.

You Can Advance to the Next Stage When:

- You are able to cover your expenses including your minimum debt payment every month without going into a negative bank balance or having to go into more debt to cover your expenses.

AN EXPLORER EXAMPLE

Toya finds herself living paycheck to paycheck. Her income never seems to be able to cover her living expenses and bills. She finds herself accumulating more debt on her credit cards rather than paying them down every month. She can barely afford the minimum payments. Toya's next step is finding ways to cover her bills and living expenses without accumulating more debt. In this stage, Toya needs to focus on getting a handle on her expenses by creating a budget and tracking what's going in and out. In this process, she may find that she is spending too much in discretionary budget categories, like going out to eat or entertainment, or she may find ways she can negotiate or reduce her mandatory expenses like insurance and internet bill. She also may find that she is not earning enough or there is a potential to earn more by picking up extra shifts at work, negotiating for higher pay, or doing something quickly for extra cash, like selling clothes or items from home or starting a side gig.

Note that I didn't make reference to Toya's income. You can be an Explorer living paycheck to paycheck whether you have a low or high income. If your total living expenses are more than your income, you fall into this stage. That said, if you have a higher income and your problem is mainly overspending, getting out of this stage will be relatively easy compared to someone who is earning a lower income that barely covers the most basic living expenses. You will be able to assess whether or not you have a true income problem or expenses problem in Chapter 8, when you create your FI plan and have to look at your numbers.

 **CADET STAGE**

> ## YOUR MAIN MISSION:
> ### Become Consumer Debt-Free

Your Current Financial Situation:
- You have consumer debt
(credit card, personal loans, car loans,
and other high interest rate debts).
- You may feel overwhelmed by your debt payments
and are only able to pay the minimum each month.

What You Should Be Working On:
- Finding room in your budget to pay more
than just the minimum debt payments.
- Having some money in your budget to save and/or invest.

You Can Advance to the Next Stage When:
You are consumer debt-free.

A CADET EXAMPLE

Meghan is able to pay her living expenses and her minimum debt payments. She's not necessarily racking up more credit card debt every month, but she's not making a lot of headway in paying it down faster than the credit card payoff schedule. If she sticks to paying the minimum, she will be in debt for most of her adult life. Meghan's next steps are to find room in her budget to pay above the minimum debt payments, start investing if she hasn't already, or continue to invest an amount of her income that feels reasonable.

 # AVIATOR STAGE

YOUR MAIN MISSION:
Become Financially Secure
by Growing Investments

Your Current Financial Situation:

- You don't have any debt outside of strategically held debt like a mortgage, low-interest student loans, or credit cards you pay off every month.

What You Should Be Working On:

- Having a fully funded emergency fund for six months to a year and FU fund.
- Investing consistently and growing your assets.

You Can Advance to the Next Stage When:

- You have enough money saved and invested and are on track to hit your standard retirement numbers and other FI goals. You may choose to settle into "coast FI" mode.
- You are in a position to leave a job or take a break from traditional work if you want.

AN AVIATOR EXAMPLE

Ann has managed to pay off her consumer debt. Any credit card debt that she does have is because she uses it to accumulate travel rewards and can pay it off every month. She has some investments but not enough that could cover her living expenses indefinitely. Ann's goal in this level is to save more into her FU fund so she can take some time off work in a couple of years to travel and invest more.

FU fund stands for "f**k you fund." It is a financial safety net that provides you with the freedom to quit your job or walk away from a situation you find unfulfilling or unpleasant. The idea is that by having an FU fund, you can maintain your independence and make decisions that prioritize your own well-being rather than feeling trapped in a job or situation due to financial constraints. How much you need in your FU fund depends on your individual circumstances. For example, one person may feel that they need to have one year's worth of expenses saved up to cover a transition, whereas another person may say they need five years' worth of expenses to cover their lifestyle while taking a break or pursuing something else without having to worry about money.

Coast FI is a concept that involves reaching a point where you have enough in your investment accounts to cover your expenses in traditional retirement, assuming the funds are left to grow over time without any further contributions. The term "coast" refers to the idea that once you have reached this point, you can "coast" toward a traditional retirement age of sixty-five without necessarily having to continue to invest aggressively, if at all. When you reach Coast FI, you can choose to shift your focus from investing for the future to spending in the now and covering current lifestyle expenses. This gives you more flexibility in what career you choose and lowers the amount of income you need.

For example, Michelle is thirty years old and wants to figure out if she is Coast FI (has enough in her retirement accounts at the standard retirement age of sixty-five). That means she has thirty-five more years for her money to grow. She assumes a portfolio growth rate of 6% and her FI number is $1,000,000. How much does she need today at thirty years old in order to consider herself Coast FI? Let's do the calculation.

Here's how you determine a Coast FI number:

- Current Age or Desired Age to Reach Coast FI—30 years old
- Years Until standard age of 65—35 years
- FI number—$1,000,000
- Expected Rate of Return—6%

Coast FI number / (1+ expected interest rate) ^ years left to standard retirement

$$1,000,000 / (1.06) \wedge 35 =$$
$$(1.06) \wedge 35 = 7.68608679231$$
$$1,000,0000 / 7.68608679231 = 130,000$$

Michelle would need $130,000 by age thirty to consider herself Coast FI. If she wanted to look into the future and see how much she'd need by age forty to be Coast FI, she could do this calculation:

- Current Age or Desired Age to Reach Coast FI—40 years old
- Years Until standard age of 65—25 years
- FI number—$1,000,000
- Expected Rate of Return—6%

$$1,000,000 / (1.06) \wedge 25 =$$
$$(1.06) \wedge 25 = 4.29187071974$$
$$1,000,0000 / 4.29187071974 = 232,998$$

Michelle would need $232,998 by age forty to consider herself Coast FI.

 COMMANDER STAGE

> ## YOUR MAIN MISSION:
> ### Become Financially Secure by Growing Investments

Your Current Financial Situation:

- You are focused on building and preserving assets.
- You have enough financial security to take extended time off work, choose what you do for work, take a lower paying job, or work part-time. (At the time of writing this book, I'm at this stage!)

What You Should Be Working On:

- Continuing to invest and enjoying the freedom that comes with financial security.
- Choosing work you love to do and that offers purpose and fulfillment.

You Can Advance to the Next Stage When:

- You have reached your FI number (25x your desired annual expenses).

A COMMANDER EXAMPLE

Jessica has reached a level where work becomes flexible. She hasn't reached her FI target number yet but is on track to retire comfortably at the standard retirement age and can take a break from traditional employment if she chooses.

Jessica may want to travel, start a business, or continue to work, knowing that at any moment, if she wanted to, she could walk away. She becomes focused on fine-tuning what she really wants and the trade-off for her preferred lifestyle vs. working longer to achieve complete FI. She may decide that working longer and retiring at the standard retirement age is worth it if she can live the lifestyle she wants. Or she may realize that working longer and needing to bring in active income is not worth it, so she makes some concessions in her lifestyle, like moving to a low cost of living area or becoming more frugal in certain areas.

 # CAPTAIN STAGE

YOUR MAIN MISSION:
Enjoy Complete Financial Independence

Your Current Financial Situation:
- You made it! You don't have to work and can live the way you want to by withdrawing 4%* of your investments or from another source of passive income.

What You Should Be Working On:
- Choosing work or other fulfilling activities you love and that offer purpose and fulfillment. Since you don't need to earn money in this stage, you can do what you truly want.
- Focusing on preserving your wealth and reassessing the amounts you'll need to keep being FI without running out of money.

* The 4% rule is explained in-depth on pages 165–166.

A CAPTAIN EXAMPLE

Keisha has reached complete FI and can live off her investments. She can choose to keep working, volunteer, or enjoy a life of leisure. She can decide what to do with her money—continue to invest or not, donate money to charity, and so forth. Keisha may have to check in with her spending and life choices to make sure she is still aligned with them and is focused on enjoying her life.

YOU'RE ALREADY ON THE JOURNEY

We are all on a financial independence journey whether we are aware of it or not. You can find yourself at a certain stage of the journey unknowingly because of past decisions you've made, not understanding how they would impact where you are today. Before I even knew what financial independence was—let's call this my Before Awareness of Financial Independence (BAFI) life, I knew money was important and that I wanted enough of it to live a happy and stable life. The younger I was, the more hopeful and ambitious I was with what I wanted from my life. Because of my ambitions, I did make some sound financial decisions that helped give me a head start when I intentionally started my journey, my After Awareness of Financial Independence life (AAFI).

HOW LONG WILL IT TAKE TO MOVE THROUGH THE STAGES?

It may be possible for you to quickly move up or even leapfrog to a more advanced stage in a relatively short amount of time. When I first heard about FI in 2014, I was operating at a Cadet level. I had student loan debt and did not have a lot of investments, but I had a good income and owned my condo along with my primary home with Woody. When it came time to get serious about my journey, I was able to move up to the Aviator stage fast by using my bonus to pay off my student loan debt and any other small credit card balances I had. Plus, I budgeted cash flow to prioritize investing over spending on discretionary expenses. I had other benefits, like a partner with a stable income and reasonable spending habits. So in many ways, I started off at a privileged position— one I worked hard to get to but was no less a privilege. That starting point explains how we were able to save and invest $169,000 in two years once I aggressively decided to pursue financial independence.

The length of time it takes you to get through each stage depends on many factors:

- your previous choices,

- the current components of your FI formula (income, expenses, mindset, and habits, which you'll learn about in the next chapter),

- your desired objectives, and

- external factors beyond your influence like the market, emergencies, or life changes that cause you to pivot.

We all travel through the stages at different rates and that's okay. Even if you are in the same Journeyer stage as someone else, because of all the factors I just mentioned, your situation can look totally different. No stage looks the same for each person. There's no such thing as a one-size-fits-all journey.

You can have two people who are Cadets in the debt payoff stage, but the length of time it takes for one person to get out of debt vs. the other is drastic because of their income, expenses, and overall life goals.

For example, if Alyssa has $40,000 in debt and an income of $50,000 and has a hard time finding extra room in her budget to pay more off her debt, then it would take her longer to pay it off than it would for Monique, who also has a $40,000 debt but a $90,000 salary and is able to find more room in her budget. Alyssa may need to focus more of her effort and time on increasing her income which may take a couple of years so her time in the Cadet stage may be longer. But she can still get there.

Don't compare yourself to other people. What matters is where *you* are starting and understanding that in each stage, there is a level of freedom. Each debt paid off, each $100 invested, matters. It unlocks a different level of freedom for you. Fewer obligations, more power over where your dollars go, the ability to say no to jobs or walk away because you have more autonomy than you did before. If you are in the Cadet stage you may be tempted to say, "I can't be happy until I'm debt-free." I have a big problem with that. Huge, actually. There's so much you can be happy for at that stage. Every time you pay off a debt, that's one less person (or institution) that you owe. Every time you pay down a debt, you are freeing up money to invest and enjoy your life. And every single time you make a payment, you reduce the stress that often accompanies unwanted debt.

For example, Veronique from episode 109 of the podcast went from living paycheck to paycheck in the Explorer stage

YOUR JOURNEY TO FINANCIAL FREEDOM   53

to the Cadet Stage in four months. As a sign language interpreter and part-time Zumba instructor, she had been living paycheck to paycheck for a while and was struggling to save or invest. Once Veronique decided to be intentional about her finances, her financial situation began to turn around. She learned how to budget, set specific financial goals, and manage her cash flow. This, along with improving her confidence through listening to podcasts, reading books, and joining my membership community, led her to ask for a raise at her job. With all of these improvements, she was able to start paying off debt and saving 20% of her income.

Acknowledging and appreciating the freedom you get on the journey—at every stage—is more important than what stage you're in or how far away you are from FI. The happiness we have in our lives is ultimately based on our internal perspective, not how many zeros are on the bank statement.

3

THE 6 ESSENTIAL COMPONENTS TO WORK ON TO REACH FI

To achieve financial independence or any other of the financial goals you've set for yourself, you'll need to understand all six of the components of what I call the FI formula. I'll get into how the formula works in Chapter 4, but for now let's take a look at the six components that you'll need to work on to help you reach your financial independence:

- Income

- Expenses

- Liabilities

- Assets

- Mindset

- Habits

The first four components—income, expenses, liabilities, and assets—capture all the quantifiable and tangible things you need to focus on with your money to reach your financial and lifestyle goals. The last two components, mindset and habits, are more intangible and can't always be measured in numbers but still impact the length of time, quality, and happiness of your journey.

All six components have their own goals. You want to improve your mindset and habits, increase income, optimize expenses, reduce liabilities, and grow your assets. (In Part 3 of the book, I give you tips on how to do this.)

THE 4 TANGIBLE COMPONENTS

Understanding the four key components of income, expenses, liabilities, and assets is crucial for anyone who wants to achieve their financial and lifestyle goals. By paying attention to these four components, you can make informed decisions about how to allocate your resources and work toward your financial objectives.

Income is the inflow of money and cash from your job, business, and investments.

Expenses are the outflow of money and cash directed to needs (mandatory expenses) and wants (discretionary expenses).

Liabilities are things you owe—credit card debt, student loan debt, personal loans, etc.

Assets are things you own—cash, investment account balances, etc.

In the upcoming chapters, we will dive into each of the four quantifiable components one at a time. I will guide you on how to evaluate your current situation with each com ponent and provide strategies for improvement. Specifically, you will learn how to increase your income, optimize your expenses, decrease your liabilities, and grow your assets. By mastering these components, you can make progress toward achieving your financial and lifestyle goals.

THE 2 INTANGIBLE COMPONENTS

The four tangible components are pretty straightforward and because they can be calculated as concrete numbers, people tend to focus on them first, especially when trying to make changes to their finances. Meanwhile the two intangibles, mindset and habits, are more subtle in how they impact you but are equally, if not more, crucial to your success. We will talk more about mindset and habits in Chapter 5, but we'll discuss it briefly here first. The intangible factors make the tangible possible. The quality of your mindset and habits allows you to enjoy the journey and impacts every single tangible component too. If you work on the four tangible components without addressing the two intangible habits you may find yourself stuck, moving slower than you'd like and feeling just plain miserable no matter how much money is in your investment accounts.

Your **mindset** is how you view the world—your thoughts and the internal set point that guides how you see things. It's how you mentally interpret events and situations.

Your **habits** are the things you do consistently, the rituals and routines that can help you on your financial journey.

At every stage of the financial journey, you will need to work through unavoidable events outside of your control, which can lead to doubt or fear. When that voice in your head tells you that you'll never get out of debt or don't deserve to earn more, you'll need to be able to recognize it but ignore it and keep moving forward. To achieve this you must prioritize your overall mindset and habits and then the specific thoughts, feelings, and behaviors that impact your finances.

In the next chapter, I'll dive further into the interplay between all six components (the four tangible and two intangible components). Then, in Part 3 of the book, as we explore each tangible component of Income, Expenses, Assets, and Liabilities, I will discuss strategies to enhance your mindset and habits associated with each specific component.

4

THE FI FORMULA AND
HOW THE 6 COMPONENTS WORK TOGETHER

The FI formula is something I came up with to show the relationship between the six components needed to reach Financial Independence. The last thing I want you to have to do is remember another formula, so don't worry, you won't have to memorize this or make it part of your daily routine. It's simply meant to demonstrate the order and importance of each component as they work together.

Remember the six components of the FI formula:

- Income
- Expenses
- Liabilities
- Assets
- Mindset
- Habits

Now it's time to put them together to see how they work, as we learn more about each one and their role in the FI formula.

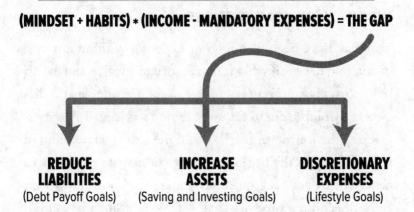

FI FORMULA

(MINDSET + HABITS) * (INCOME - MANDATORY EXPENSES) = THE GAP

REDUCE LIABILITIES	INCREASE ASSETS	DISCRETIONARY EXPENSES
(Debt Payoff Goals)	(Saving and Investing Goals)	(Lifestyle Goals)

THE THREE MAIN FI FORMULA CONCEPTS

First, let's go over the three main concepts that are critical to your success in working the FI formula:

- Your expenses must be divided into two broad categories: mandatory expenses and discretionary expenses. This helps establish their order and priority.

- What the gap is, and why increasing it allows you to reach FI without completely sacrificing your desired lifestyle.

- Your income is the most dominant of all the tangible components and serves four main purposes: (1) cover your mandatory expenses; (2) pay off your liabilities; (3) increase your assets; and (4) pay for discretionary expenses. The priority of these purposes varies depending on your Journeyer level.

CONCEPT 1: MANDATORY EXPENSES VS. DISCRETIONARY EXPENSES

You may have been paying your expenses without any real distinction between what is mandatory to survive and earn a living (paying your rent/mortgage or for gas) and what is discretionary (going out to eat, subscription services). To progress through the Journeyer levels, you'll need to separate them in your budget. In the beginning stages, it may be necessary to be strict and cut back on discretionary expenses. However, as you become more financially stable, you may be able to allow for some discretionary expenses that you deem non-negotiables. For instance, a gym membership may be a discretionary expense in the early stages, but as you progress, it may be something you prioritize and make room for in your budget by earning more, cutting back in other areas, or adjusting your debt payoff timeline. It is important to note that being in the Explorer or Cadet stage does not necessarily mean you have to completely eliminate your gym membership if it holds value and brings you happiness. You can and should include discretionary expenses in your spending that align with your values and bring you joy, regardless of your stage. However, it is crucial to understand the distinction between discretionary and essential expenses and make informed decisions about how your spending choices impact your progress through the various stages.

CONCEPT 2: THE GAP

The gap is the difference between your income and mandatory expenses. How you handle the gap is how you get ahead financially. You use the gap to pay down debt, increase assets, and pay for your discretionary expenses. For the income side of the equation the goal is to maximize or increase your income level. The expenses component is meant to be *optimized*, not necessarily minimized to its smallest number. You want to eliminate excess spending on things that aren't a priority for you. The purpose is to increase the difference between your income and your mandatory expenses—that is, to increase your gap. The larger the gap, the faster you'll be able to reach your goals.

You have the option to either find more of a financial gap or create one. Finding more space in the gap can be mind-blowing because you don't necessarily have to make any significant modifications to your income or expenses. It could be as simple as canceling a subscription you don't use or re-organizing your spending. Alternatively, you can create more gap by taking more decisive action, such as finding a higher-paying job or deliberately reducing an expense you enjoy. I believe that a lot of people have hidden money right within their reach, which they can easily uncover without making significant sacrifices or putting in too much effort.

Let's look at an example of how increasing the gap can help you accelerate a debt payoff plan. For instance, paying an additional $300 toward your debt on a monthly basis can shave three years off of your debt payoff timeline.

Example 1: Using Gap to Pay Off Debt: $10,000 Credit Card, 19% Interest Rate

Find no extra gap—keep things the same and pay minimum payment of $200 per month	Find additional $100 to put toward debt per month payoff for a total of $300 monthly payments	Find additional $200 to put toward debt per month payoff for a total of $400 monthly payments	Find additional $300 to put toward debt per month payoff for a total of $500 monthly payments
Pay off in 60 months	Pay off in 50 months	Pay off in 30 months	Pay off in 24 months

If we look at utilizing your gap to invest more, you can see that finding an additional $300 to invest can result in a having almost $50,000 more at the end of 10 years vs. not investing at all.

Example 2: Using Gap to Invest: Starting with $500, 10 Years of Growth, 6% Interest Rate

Find no extra gap—keep things the same no investments per month	Find additional $100 to invest per month	Find additional $200 invest per month	Find additional $300 to invest per month
Balance: $910	Balance: $17,298	Balance: $33,686	Balance: 50,074

As you can see, if you increase your gap and choose to put it toward a financial goal like paying off debt or investing, it can take you far.

CONCEPT 3: INCOME'S 4 PURPOSES

Your income is the dominant tangible component and it determines the speed at which you reach your goals and the quality of the journey. Income makes it possible to live the lifestyle you want today and pursue long-term goals like FI.

Income is your Net Income after taxes and any pre-tax retirement investing is taken out of your check. It's essentially your take home pay. You will need to keep this in mind in setting investing goals because you may be already contributing to a 401(k) which reduces take home pay and allows you to save on taxes.

Your income serves four purposes:

- Pays for Mandatory Expenses

- Reduces Liabilities

- Increases Assets

- Pays for Discretionary Expenses

You need sufficient income to take care of all four things. If FI is your mission, you'll want to eventually build up enough assets to generate enough income to cover your expenses.

Most people spend their income as follows:

HOW MOST PEOPLE
SPEND THEIR INCOME

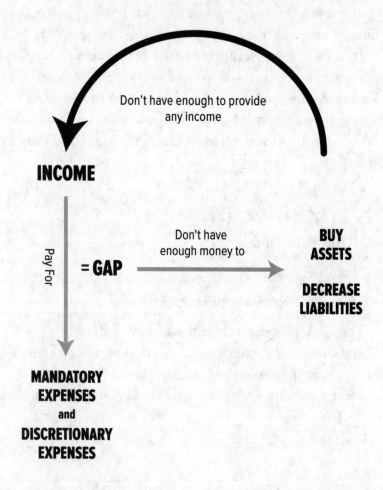

Don't have enough to provide
any income

INCOME

Pay For

= GAP → Don't have
enough money to

**BUY
ASSETS**

**DECREASE
LIABILITIES**

**MANDATORY
EXPENSES**
and
**DISCRETIONARY
EXPENSES**

Mandatory and discretionary expenses are given the same
priority. What's left over at the end of the month, if anything,
is what they use to pay the minimum of their debt while still
accumulating more debt. Investing and buying assets is an after-

thought or nice idea but not a priority. Essentially, the majority of their income is spent on expenses, and the rest goes to dealing with minimum debt payments and maybe buying assets. As their income increases, so do their expenses. The priority is in the now and living life today, while the future is an afterthought.

Instead, here's the way you should look at how to use your income:

HOW TO SPEND INCOME TO REACH FI

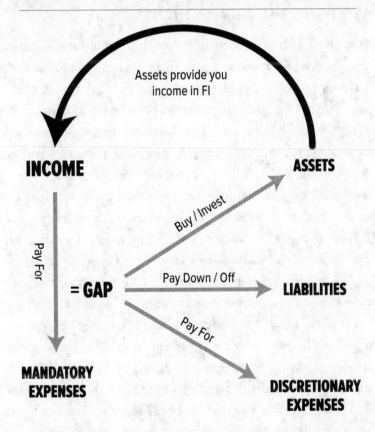

Assets provide you
income in FI

INCOME   ASSETS

Pay For

Buy / Invest

= GAP   Pay Down / Off   LIABILITIES

Pay For

MANDATORY
EXPENSES

DISCRETIONARY
EXPENSES

To reach financial independence, you must reorganize your spending priorities. Income should first be used to pay for mandatory expenses, then to reduce liabilities and increase assets, and last, to pay for discretionary expenses.

The key is to find the balance of spending your income in a way that takes care of you both today and tomorrow. This involves a shift in your relationship to time and the benefits you get today from things you need to do for the future.

WORKING THE 6 COMPONENTS

Reaching financial independence requires a holistic approach that involves all aspects of your financial life and the six components: income, expenses, assets, liabilities, habits, and mindset. Think of these components as the building blocks of a house, with income and assets forming the foundation, expenses and liabilities forming the roof, and habits and mindset forming the walls. When all of these components are strong and work together, you can create a financially resilient and stable "house" that can withstand external factors like job layoffs or recessions. However, if any component is weak, it can compromise the stability of your overall financial situation.

A wonderful example of someone who embraced the journey and is doing as much as she can is Cassandra, who was on episode 111 of the podcast. When I first met her, she was a podcast listener who contacted me to give her one-on-one money coaching. She eventually joined my membership program too. Cassandra desperately wanted to improve her financial situation. But as a teacher burdened with student loans, she faced difficulties in making progress financially.

To achieve her desired outcome, Cassandra realized that

she had to work on all six areas of the FI formula. She created a budget to manage and prioritize her expenses, and she explored additional opportunities to leverage her teaching skills. As a result, Cassandra was able to bring in an extra $10,000 in one year by becoming an after-school program assistant. She has had about $25,000 of her student loans paid off through the federal teacher forgiveness programs and is currently teaching first grade at an American international school in Abu Dhabi—something she couldn't have envisioned before starting her financial independence journey.

Also, building and maintaining a strong financial house is an ongoing process that requires consistent attention, effort, and time. You won't be able to build the strongest, biggest house overnight.

In a perfect world, we would be able to work on all six components of financial independence at the same time. However, the world is not perfect and neither are we. Therefore, it's important to give yourself grace and set a realistic timeline for progress. If you're in a season of life where you can only focus on one or two components at a time, that's okay. For example, if you are a contract worker or earning minimum wage and unable to cut back on expenses, your main focus should be increasing income. This may involve finding a more stable job or a better income-producing opportunity. You may not be able to pay down debt or invest as much right away, but that's alright, you are still making progress on your journey to financial independence.

When it comes to money, we often focus on how the money we have now helps us now. And that makes sense if you're working with a limited amount of money today, because it doesn't yet feel like it can be stretched to make both the present version of you and the future version of you happy. But by creating more of a gap as you improve mindsets and habits, increase income, and optimize expense, you'll begin to create more cash flow to provide a good life for yourself now and a good life for yourself in the future.

PRIORITIZING THE 4 PURPOSES OF INCOME BY JOURNEYER STAGE

I introduced the gap as the difference between your income and mandatory expenses. Now let's see how you will use the gap to reach your goals. After paying for your mandatory expenses, you need to divide the leftover money into three categories:

- Paying Off Debt
- Growing/Maintaining Assets (Savings and Investments)
- Paying for Discretionary Expenses

The chart below generalizes your spending priorities according to your Journeyer stage.

THE JOURNEYER PRIORITIES CHART

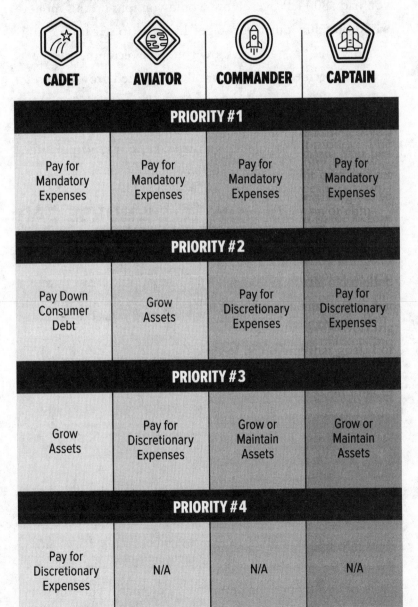

CADET	AVIATOR	COMMANDER	CAPTAIN
PRIORITY #1			
Pay for Mandatory Expenses	Pay for Mandatory Expenses	Pay for Mandatory Expenses	Pay for Mandatory Expenses
PRIORITY #2			
Pay Down Consumer Debt	Grow Assets	Pay for Discretionary Expenses	Pay for Discretionary Expenses
PRIORITY #3			
Grow Assets	Pay for Discretionary Expenses	Grow or Maintain Assets	Grow or Maintain Assets
PRIORITY #4			
Pay for Discretionary Expenses	N/A	N/A	N/A

NOTE: The Explorer category is excluded because the main priority of the Explorer is to pay for your mandatory expenses.

Let's say that after you paid for your mandatory expenses, you had $800 left over. How would you split up this money based on your Journeyer stage? In order to streamline and simplify this, I'm going to show you some recommended percentages (see below). Note that I've separated growing assets into two different categories, saving and investing. The tables below show how to break out spending after you've paid for your mandatory expenses, so things like your rent/mortgage and groceries are already covered.

EXAMPLE OF HOW TO DISBURSE GAP BY JOURNEYER STAGE
To Reach Financial & Lifestyle Goals

JOURNEYER LEVEL	Cadet	Aviator	Commander	Captain
Debt Payoff	50%			
Savings	20%	30%		
Investing	20%	50%	50%	
Discretionary Expenses	10%	20%	50%	100%
SUM:	100%	100%	100%	100%

NOTE: The Explorer category is excluded because the main priority of the Explorer is to pay for your mandatory expenses.

Based on the percentages, this is how you would spend that leftover $800, according to each Journeyer stage. Please note that the way the money is divided is an example of prioritizing where you put your money and how much you can split up the additional cash flow.

JOURNEYER LEVEL	Cadet	Aviator	Commander	Captain
Debt Payoff*	$400	$0	$0	$0
Savings	$160	$240	$0	$0
Investing	$160	$400	$400	$0
Discretionary Expenses	$80	$160	$400	$800

* Paying off debt above the minimum.

NOTE: The Explorer category is excluded because the main priority of the Explorer is to pay for your mandatory expenses.

In the Explorer stage you are focused on paying your bills, so the only priority is to cover your mandatory expenses. While you most likely will have discretionary expenses and minimum debt payments, the goal is to increase income and/or decrease overall expenses until you hit stability.

In the Cadet stage, your priority is paying off consumer debt, but you still should invest and find room for discretionary spending, to help balance out the journey.

In the Aviator stage, your consumer debt is paid off so you can focus on growing assets and increase your spending on discretionary income.

In the Commander stage, you've reached a comfortable place with your investments. Maybe this is your end point and early retirement is not for you, so you decide to slow down on investing aggressively and to spend more in discretionary expenses (e.g., split the $800 equally between investing and discretionary spending). Or maybe you have a goal of reaching financial independence sooner rather than later and still want to focus on investing aggressively instead of on discretionary spending (e.g., $600 investing and $200 discretionary split).

In the Captain stage, you've reached financial independence, so you can choose to work or just use your investments to pay your mandatory and discretionary expenses.

As you move through the Journeyer stages, you gain more flexibility and are able to spend more of your money the way you want. That's something to look forward to that will help motivate you along the way.

HOW INTENSE DO YOU WANT TO GET?

While you can go to the extreme to reach your goals—making the most money possible while spending the least money possible—you need to consider the trade-offs and quality of life you want to have during the process. For example, you may not want to have bare-bones expenses and cut out discretionary spending to meet your goals faster, just like you may not want to work overtime or start a side hustle outside of your nine-to-five to supplement your income. But if you are reading this and you are not financially where you want to be and don't think you are on track to reach your goals or financial independence, then you *must* work on the components of the FI formula. Otherwise, you'll stay in the same position you are in now.

The intensity at which you work to improve the components of your FI formula can also depend on your Journeyer level. If you're an Explorer or Cadet, you may need to actively work more at increasing your income and monitoring your expenses, so you can reach the Aviator, Commander, or Captain stage, where it's possible to ease up on the intensity. The higher the Journeyer level, the more flexibility you have.

For some people, seeing results with their FI formula and increasing the gap is as simple as cutting out budget items that don't matter to them and being more thoughtful about their expenses. For example, Marie looks through her spending and finds that she can save at least $200 by bringing her lunch to work at least three times a week and making breakfast at home. Marie usually doesn't even enjoy the lunch she buys out, but it's convenient. Taking time to prepare a sandwich and salad the night before and eating breakfast at home doesn't feel like she's losing out on anything, so reallocating $200 in her budget to get out of debt faster is a no-brainer.

For others, maybe increasing their income is not as difficult. You may have a unique skill set that you can easily earn more money from or be in a profession that has a clear path to earning a better salary. Sandra works at a restaurant but loves to draw and considers herself an artist at heart. She realizes she can offer her services to do in-home kid art classes or parties to earn more money. Combining her love for art and earning extra money feels good, and drawing is a skill she already possesses, so she doesn't have to spend time learning how to do it. Sandra already works at a location where she can hang up fliers and has access to parent and neighborhood Facebook groups where she can post about her services. By starting to advertise her side hustle, she finds a few customers and can earn up to $300 extra a month by offering her services on the side.

Years ago, I was clueless about the world of financial independence and had no idea this was a pathway to the freedom I'd been yearning for. I had a lot to learn, and I'm still learning more every day. Understanding these concepts and the way they work together was an important and necessary step on my journey—and it's critical for your journey too.

Part 1: The What, Why & How of Financial Independence Checklist

- [ ] Understand the concepts of Financial Independence and Financial Freedom

- [ ] Discover Your Current Journeyer Stage

- [ ] Know the 4 Tangible Components of the FI Formula

- [ ] Know the 2 Intangible Components of the FI Formula

PART 2:

CREATING YOUR ENJOYABLE
FINANCIAL INDEPENDENCE PLAN

5

ASSESSING YOUR MINDSET AND HABITS

Before we get started on looking at the numbers and creating a plan for how you will reach FI, it's important to focus on doing the inner work, understanding where you currently are with your mindset and habits. Without working on these foundational elements, it will be difficult to create a clear vision for your future. This chapter will guide you through an assessment of where you currently stand and provide you with tools to help eliminate any limiting beliefs and improve your habits, so that you can ultimately create the best life for yourself.

MINDSET

Your mindset is a combination of your internal beliefs and thoughts, which determines your relationship with the external world, other people, and yes, money. Your mindset is shaped by various influences and is always evolving and changing. When you are born, your mindset is like a pile of untouched clay. Then imagine hands beginning to shape it and leave their mark—your environment, parents and family, society, culture, and then your own experiences as you grow up. Life becomes an experiment where you observe cause and effect. Things happen all around you that you learn to make sense of and interpret. Naturally, there will be many things outside of your control that will happen to you as well as those within your control. How you react to these things, especially the things that set you back or seem like obstacles, is important. Do you view obstacles and setbacks as signals to give up or do you look at them as opportunities to learn, pivot to something else, or try again?

Also, having a positive mindset isn't the same as having a false sense of reality. I'm not asking you to pretend everything is okay and not have moments of doubt. There will be times when you want to give in and rest on this pathway—and in fact, rest and ease is the ultimate goal, but I don't want you to completely give up. When you have a positive mindset it creates a more enjoyable journey to your goals. In order to understand where you currently are with your mindset, you will have to be introspective and honest with yourself. Peeling back the layers to check out the foundation of who you are can be scary but it's necessary.

We can't target your money mindset without looking at your overall mindset. If you don't quite feel you are where you need to be on your financial journey—and let's face it: all of us, including me, feel that way at certain times—then it's most likely a symptom of your overall mindset and there are other areas in your life where you feel the same discomfort.

★ ★ ★

Years ago at a baby shower, I ran into an old friend who briefly mentioned a recent eleven-day silent meditation retreat she had attended. Intrigued, I asked for more information and looked up the retreat—Vipassana Meditation—on their website. I was drawn to the idea of meditating in silence all day. And did I mention it was completely free? So I found a center in Massachusetts and signed up for the next available session. I knew there was always something more to this life than waking up, commuting to work, and sitting behind a desk doing what felt like work that didn't matter in the grand scheme of things.

We are often so busy and time poor that we never get a chance to really see and experience the richness that life has to offer. This eleven-day silent meditation retreat was a chance to slow down, disconnect from everyone, and reconnect with myself. Soon enough, I found myself at the retreat center. We meditated for eight hours a day, got up at 5:00 a.m., and only ate vegetarian meals. Each meditation session was one hour to two hours long. We were taught to observe without judgment what is called "the monkey mind," referring to the restless and wandering state of the mind that is full of distractions, worries, and thoughts that constantly jump from one thing to another, like a monkey jumping from branch to branch. Stillness, quiet, calm were the only goals for the day. Looking back, it was one of the rare times in my adult life where I felt so at peace having no responsibilities and material possessions, but yet I felt so, so much abundance. The facilities were clean but basic; the food was simple; there were no luxuries of the physical kind. Time moved slower. I got a peek into what life could look like without the distractions and expectations from others. It was life-changing. There was so much more to explore within me, in the world, and I wasn't going to let my job or money stand in the way of living my authentic life.

But once the retreat was over and I returned to the real world, despite my best efforts to continue my daily meditation practice, I was unable to keep it up and eventually fell back into my everyday routine of commuting and working. Despite not being able to keep up my meditation practice, I learned something important in my time at the retreat. Eleven days of silence taught me that the deepest journey I could embark on is the one I take inward.

There are so many depths within us that make us who we are. Our mind is powerful beyond what we can comprehend. We live in a world that prioritizes busyness, outward action, and physical possessions. It's hard to figure out who we truly are and what we truly want if we are always on the go commuting to work, rushing to a meeting, scrolling on social media.

You may not have eleven days to dedicate to being silent. I have yet to find the time to go back and do it again. But taking *any* amount of time to yourself—to be deliberate about observing, and acknowledging without judgment who we are and what we want—is important on your financial independence and life journey.

HABITS

Habits are also an important factor in your financial journey. Your habits are either helping and supporting you or hindering you. Your ability to save or reach your financial goals strongly correlates to whether or not you have good habits. For example, habits to help you with your expenses can include meal prepping to help you save money or budgeting that can help you stick to your spending goals.

Anything that you do often or consistently can be considered a habit. Some habits are so ingrained in our everyday life that we don't even consider them habits—they are just things that we do. Brushing your teeth every morning is a habit. Drinking coffee every day or eating a certain snack is a habit. Our habits make up the activities in our lives. Choosing to do or not do something consistently over a period of time will affect the quality of your daily life and overall life. With some habits you don't see the effect until days, weeks, or years later and with some habits you see the impact immediately. The same way your money grows and compounds over time when you invest it is the same way the results you ultimately want to have are the product of compounding good habits.

MINDSET AND HABITS WORKING TOGETHER

Habits and mindset go hand in hand because oftentimes we'll need to shift our mindset around a topic before we can begin to build better habits around it. Or the reverse can be true where we have to begin to do a task and with action comes more clarity, knowledge, and results leading to a more favorable mindset around the subject. This is especially true when it comes to money. I believe one of the reasons people have such an aversion to dealing with their money or starting their journey is because the habits required to become

successful require things from you that feel more like obligations, the "responsible" things where the result and benefit
feel far away. The habits of investing, saving money, budgeting, making more economical spending choices, etc., are all
meant to make us financially secure in the future vs. giving
us joy doing what we want in the moment. Not only do we
feel obligated to work on things we don't really want to do
and pay bills that we don't want to pay, on top of that we have
to do all the other things that feel like they're taking away
from our fun and joy. Earning, spending, and managing our
money feels like a chore with minimum upfront return and if
you don't like the way you make money (you hate your job)
or the way you have to spend money (you hate paying bills),
then managing and growing your money (creating a budget
or investing for the long term) feels like another weight you
need to carry on top of an already unbearable load. It can be
overwhelming and unfulfilling because of the lack of joy in
the process. Money feels like just a means to an end. We want
to have more money so that we can be comfortable and live
the life we want. To be a consistent winner or reap the ultimate rewards of money, we need to become better money
managers for today and tomorrow and develop the mindset
and habits that will help us achieve our goals. We need to
balance the wants and needs that we have today vs. the wants
and needs for our future. This is no small task, it's hard to do
the things you need to do today to succeed if you don't see
the results you want right away. This is why working on our
mindset and habits around money is crucial to seeing success.

MINDSET

ASSESSING YOUR OVERALL MINDSET

Without understanding how your mindset and habits feed into your current financial situation you can't begin to make the necessary changes to reach your future financial success. If you have a hard time spending money in a way that supports your goals or are underearning, there are most likely some mindset work and habit changes you can make to progress in these areas. Without working on the intangible factors, you won't be able to make sustainable changes or progress.

If you want to get a true sense of where you currently are with your mindset, observing and just becoming aware of your thoughts and feelings is important. You don't have to do anything at first but bring awareness to your ongoing thoughts and the internal dialogue you have with yourself on a daily basis.

Have you ever started singing a song you don't even like, but you know all the lyrics because it's catchy and you feel like you've heard it a million times? Your lips start moving, and soon you're singing along without even realizing it. Your internal thoughts can be like that, at times narrating and repeating negative patterns without you being conscious of them. Is your internal record repeating the same snarky or negative song? You may not have realized you have been singing along, but if you can catch yourself doing it you can choose to sing along with it or change the tune. Author John Acuff, who was also on episode 236 of the podcast, wrote about this in his book *Soundtracks: The Surprising Solution to*

Overthinking. Acuff calls the negative stories that we tell ourselves "broken soundtracks." They take no effort to think and are the most persuasive forms of fear because every time you listen to one, it gets easier to believe the next time. This is why simple awareness is so important. You can't do anything about it if you don't know it's happening in the first place.

BE OBSERVANT

Observe your everyday thoughts and write them down. You can do this with a journal every morning or even use your phone to record voice notes or use the notes application to jot down your thoughts. Note your thoughts without filtering or judging them.

You can also use prompts or targeted questions to help you get started. Here's a list of sample prompts:

- What comes to mind when you wake up in the morning?
- What are you excited about?
- What makes you happy?
- What makes you concerned?
- What are you grateful for?
- What do you want to change about yourself or your life?

Continue to observe how you react to people and to situations that happen throughout the day. Before you respond by acting or speaking, see what comes up for you. From here you can begin to see patterns in your thoughts and feelings.

For example, observe the thoughts you have as you enter into your workplace. Do you have a negative stream of emotions and thoughts like "X is incompetent," "They don't like me," "They never acknowledge my hard work," "There's a position open but what's the point of applying because I won't get it," or "I hate it here"? Your thoughts directly impact how you interact with your coworkers and boss in your speech, body language, and overall mood. Having negative thoughts is normal and happens. But having these thoughts all day, every day impacts your emotional/mental health, your trajectory at your job, and ultimately your income. If you can recognize your thoughts and any patterns, acknowledge them and give yourself grace for having them. You can then begin to work through improving them. Not for the sake of the coworker who truly might be annoying you, but for your own progress and happiness on your journey. The world indeed can be a sucky place; people can indeed be quite awful; the system is not set up in a way that allows you to easily win. Despite all the negativity, there is still plenty of positivity to be found. Since we have to be in this world, we might as well strive to make the most out of our experience and find joy and benefit in it.

When working at my corporate job in New Jersey, my commute was a nightmare. It would take an hour and a half each way on a good day to get to work with normal traffic. I was determined to not let the circumstance of my horrible commute ruin my mood for the day. There were so many things outside of my control when it came to the commute overall so I could only focus on how I perceived the commute and what I did with that time in the car. I quickly realized that if I got in my car with a bad attitude and negative thoughts on how the drive would be, then I would most likely have a miserable commute.

In contrast, when I approached it determined to make the best out of the situation with a more positive mindset, I had better driving days. I also made sure to try and control what I could when it came to my comfort level in the car. When I started listening to podcasts, I'd already have the ones I wanted to listen to queued up for the drive. On some mornings, I was actually, dare I say, excited to get in the car and listen to some of my favorite podcasts. Sometimes my coworkers would say, "I don't know how you do that commute every day," and I'd respond, "I just don't think about it," and I really tried not to think about it. I'd try not to focus my energy on what I hated about it, because if I did, I'd be sucked into a negativity loop that would be impossible to escape and would ooze into everything I did that day. I knew I wasn't able or willing to change my commute so instead of making it my enemy, I raised the white flag, befriended it, and turned it into my ally. This time in the car allowed me to immerse myself into the world of financial freedom and financial independence and personal development podcasts.

Once I made this powerful mindset shift from negative to positive regarding my commute, it not only made it bearable but my commute became the reason why I was able to eventually leave my job to reach the Commander Journeyer stage. Without it, I would not have found out about financial independence nor learned the art of podcasting and about entrepreneurship, all of which led me to start *Journey to Launch*.

REFLECTION QUESTIONS

Taking the time to reflect on our personal money story can help us better understand our relationship with money and identify areas for growth and improvement. The following questions are designed to encourage self-reflection and exploration, free from judgment or shame. Answer each question honestly and thoughtfully to gain valuable insights about your relationship with money.

Be truthful and answer these questions without judging yourself.

- What were some of your first money memories?

- Was money talked about in your household growing up?

- How was money discussed by your parents?

- What thoughts or feelings come to mind when you think about money? Do you feel stressed or anxious, or do you feel a sense of security and comfort?

- Do you think having more money will solve your current problems?

- When you picture someone who has a lot of money, such as a trust fund baby, how do you feel about that person?

- Do you think people who have a lot of money are good or bad?

- Is it possible for someone to be wealthy and a good person?

- Is money the root of all evil?

Once you've answered these questions, sit with your responses. Can you see a correlation with your answers to the current way you handle or avoid money? Exploring your initial reactions and responses to these prompts may provide insight into your beliefs and attitudes around money and wealth. Now is your chance to begin to rewrite and rewire your money story.

There are so many personal finance and get rich quick clickbait headlines from online publications: "Woman pays off $500,000 of debt on a $60,000 salary" or "They saved $169,000 in 2 years and only did these 3 things." That last headline was an article written about my saving story. That's how I know those simple headlines hide a lot of details.

It's easy to be critical and roll your eyes at them—and for good reason when they are pulling the most eye-catching points to make you read the article. But if you dig deeper and can see beyond the flashy title is there anything you can learn from the story? Are you only critical or do you try to find something applicable or inspirational?

I'll see people share their debt payoff or money wins online and some of the responses are "Of course it was easy for them, they had a six-figure job" or "She must have had help from her parents" or "The reason why they were able to do that is because they come from money, that doesn't apply to me." And yes, everything won't apply to you. Other people will have different advantages or have had more help, but that doesn't take away from your ability to do something extraordinary with your life too.

It's similar to me rolling my eyes when I hear someone who doesn't have the responsibility of raising small children tell me how productive they are in the mornings or how much they get done in a day. I'm like, "Of course you can, you don't have three tiny humans vying for your attention and dominating your life the way I do, so yes, it's easier for you to focus your attention!" But even with the differences in our circumstances, is there something else about their story that I could learn from? I'm open to finding out.

The same goes the other direction. I have a dear friend who is a single mom to two boys. She is able to get as much done with less support in the home compared to the support that I have with a partner. I'm always in awe of how she handles it all and salute her and other single parents doing the best they can for their children. People will always have more or less support, help, or resources than you at any given point. Everything is relative. How can you recognize your own privileges and advantages while being open to learning what applies and is helpful from other people's experiences and ignoring what doesn't?

When I first discovered the FIRE movement it was through podcasts. All of the podcasts that I started listening to were by white men. I rarely heard stories similar to mine or could relate to much of their perspective. But I didn't need to relate or connect to everything. I just needed to connect to one thing. They felt stuck in their job; I felt stuck in my job too. They enjoyed living a really frugal life and dumpster diving and getting their groceries for cheap. I didn't want to dumpster dive but wow, it made me consider what ways I could save on food costs instead. They lived on only $25,000 a year, I didn't want to live that frugally but I knew there must be a way to learn how to scale back my expenses until I reached my goals.

RETUNING AND IMPROVING YOUR MINDSET

Once you've gotten a sense of your current mindset the next step is to find ways to cultivate a more positive mindset that is helpful and conducive to your journey vs. a mindset that is limiting and impedes your journey. Let's look into some free tools and resources as well as paid and professional resources.

Podcasts

Many podcasts are free to consume and listen to. There are podcasts on literally every topic you can think of, from true crime to parenting. The information and inspiration you can learn from a podcast is boundless. There are no restrictions on how many different podcasts you can listen to and you can listen anywhere or at any time, on your commute, doing routine work, working out, taking a walk, cleaning the house. Listening to podcasts literally changed my life. I didn't know the FIRE movement existed or about people who actually ran their own businesses or traveled the world as a hobby until I discovered podcasts. It exponentially expanded my worldview. Your current world is limited to your actual physical environment, who you actually know, where you can physically travel to, and who you can talk to. To be able to listen to the life experiences and lessons from other everyday people just like you or experts on a subject you are interested in that can help you be more informed is invaluable. And did I mention almost all podcasts are FREE?! In order to prime your mind for limitless possibilities and making money, achieving success and creating the life you desired that once felt like a dream, begin listening to podcasts that show you how or inspire you that it is possible. There are many personal finance podcasts, personal development podcasts, and entrepreneurship podcasts that can help you get started.

Books

Read books on personal finance and FIRE topics. Books are low-cost, or free if borrowing from your local library, and are a good resource to learn and help set yourself up for success on your journey. Since you are already reading this book, congratulations, you are doing it!

Community/Social Connections

Surround yourself with other people who have similar goals who you can learn from and be inspired by. Finding communities—whether they're free online Facebook groups, paid online communities, inspiring social media accounts, or local community meetups—where the goals you've set for yourself and your life are encouraged and the normal vs. what feels out of place in your real world—will help to shift and evolve your mindset.

Therapy

Talking with a licensed therapist is important. I believe everyone can benefit from therapy. Therapy is a place where you can get unbiased feedback and tools to help you navigate your emotions and the world around you. Since there are various forms of therapy, you'll have to choose the one that's right for you, but overall therapy can help you assess where your current thoughts, feelings, and actions come from and help you work through them.

Coaching

Consider looking into life coaching or mindset coaching from a professional or accredited coach. Life coaching is a collaborative and forward-focused process that helps people identify their goals, overcome obstacles, and make positive changes in various areas of their lives. Mindset coaching focuses specifically on helping individuals develop a positive and growth-oriented mindset. Look for coaches who have obtained proper training and certifications from reputable coaching organizations.

TURNING A FIXED MINDSET INTO A GROWTH MINDSET

How we view or do not view opportunities and setbacks frames how we navigate the world in front of us. Do you have a fixed mindset or a growth mindset? A *fixed mindset* is the perspective that you are your failures. If you can't do something or fail at something, you see it as a sign that you are not capable of ever doing it. A *growth mindset* is the opposite. With a growth mindset, you view failure as an opportunity to improve in some way. Your inability to do something right away doesn't make you give up, but rather you are determined to figure out how to get better at it or succeed. A fixed mindset limits your life while a growth mindset expands your life's possibilities.

This doesn't mean that you want to tackle every problem

all the time or never want to give up, but when you commit to having a growth mindset then you view everything through the lens of believing it can be possible if you want it enough. You can then choose to go after a goal or thing you want or not as opposed to feeling limited to what you can accomplish based on your current circumstances and situation.

FIXED MINDSET VS. GROWTH MINDSET

This is too confusing for me to understand This is confusing, but I'm going to keep reviewing it until I understand a little more than I did yesterday

I'm not good at numbers so I won't be good with my finances Numbers sometimes confuse me, but I won't let that momentary confusion prevent me from succeeding with my finances

I don't have the connections or access like he has to get where I want to be I may not know the people yet that can help me, but I will do as much as I can to be the best I can be at this and put myself out there to meet others and I know I will find those who are meant to help me

They had help from their parents and came from money, I won't be able to do what thev did Sure, they had help and more privilege but it doesn't mean I can't succeed too

Part of expanding the possibilities for yourself and what you are capable of is realizing that you don't have to be good at everything. You don't have to be good at math or numbers to be good with money. You don't have to be the best public speaker to advocate for yourself. The idea is to be okay with not being perfect and not getting things right.

What are some areas in your life that you want to see improvements in but you've given up on because you don't feel smart or good enough? When it comes to understanding money or new concepts involving your finances do you avoid the process or keep going until you understand enough to build on your knowledge? Again, you don't have to get everything right or understand all the financial concepts in the world—you just have to be committed to learning and figuring things out.

Think back to something you once didn't understand and how you either understand it a little better or have even mastered it now. Your example doesn't have to be finance related. You weren't born knowing how to walk, talk, read, or write in your native language and yet you learned how to do those things. You can even go back to childhood to find an example.

As adults who have become accustomed to our daily routines and ruts we can go on autopilot and take the path of least resistance. Unless you are actively looking for challenges or taking on learning opportunities, most of your day is consumed with things you already know how to do in the way you've been doing them. I look at kids as they are in their active learning stages as examples of what it's like to be consistently emotionally, mentally, and physically challenged to grow and learn. Children have been learning and adapting since birth and every day they are introduced to something new that they don't know how to do yet or understand, but one day I know will be routine for them, like learning how to ride their bike, how to read, or how to play basketball. You too were once a child and didn't know how to do many of the things you're able to do today.

What are some of the areas in your life where you currently view things from a fixed mindset? Example: "I'm not good at numbers," "I'm not organized," etc. How can you view them from a growth mindset? What will you do to improve in those areas? (Reminder, you don't have to be good or want to succeed at everything you do. I for one do not consider myself a good cook, but it's because I don't want to be a good cook. I choose to not want to focus on that now, but if I know that if I did decide to put more effort into the kitchen, I could better my cooking skills.) Pick the areas you actually want to be better at or areas that if you improve in, they will greatly increase your chances of reaching your goals.

GROWTH MINDSET EXERCISE

Here's an exercise to try to flex your growth mindset muscle. Take on a new challenge that is low-risk, meaning your ultimately succeeding or failing at it does not hold too much weight for you emotionally or financially, to remind yourself what it's like to be a novice and work through something challenging. It can be something like taking up running when you previously thought you hated it. The challenge can be working yourself up to run 1 mile or run a 5k. You can decide that you want to take a beginner's level foreign language class online or search YouTube on how to begin knitting.

For me it's as simple as choosing to go to my step class at my gym, which is challenging for me because I struggle to remember the seemingly simple step combinations that the instructor and all the seasoned steppers get where they look like a choreographed dance troupe. I have to concentrate really hard to follow the right steps and I mess up often. At first, I avoided the class but now I take it as a challenge because I see improvement and a new understanding of steps that I didn't even know how to execute before.

OPERATING FROM A BE-DO-HAVE MODEL INSTEAD OF A DO-HAVE-BE MODEL

The Be-Do-Have model is a self-improvement concept that suggests that personal transformation starts with "being" a certain type of person, which leads to "doing" certain actions, and ultimately results in "having" the desired outcome. In other words, by embodying a certain identity and taking specific actions, we can achieve the outcomes we desire.

While the origin of the Be-Do-Have model is not entirely clear, it has been widely used in personal development and self-help circles since at least the 1980s. Some attribute the concept to various authors and speakers, including Zig Ziglar, T. Harv Eker, and Steven Covey, author of 7 *Habits of Highly Effective People*. The Be-Do-Have model can be applied to the single goals you have or your overall life and financial goals. For example, let's say you want to become better at cooking. Using the Be-Do-Have model, you begin to think of yourself as a cook already who is learning your craft vs. someone who doesn't like to cook and wants to be a cook. You, my friend, are already a cook, you just need more experience in the kitchen, which you begin to give yourself, which is the doing part. Maybe you do more research on the dishes you want to cook, and begin to learn the differences between different spices and flavors. Before you know it, you are the chef you set out to be, but it began first through believing you already had inside what you needed to possess to become one. The Be-Do-Have approach says inhabit the traits and mindset of the future you who has the things you want.

In the Be-Do-Have model, you don't have to wait for the goal to be achieved to receive the emotional and mental benefits from achieving it. This is especially helpful when on your financial independence journey, because while it can take a while to reach your interim goals on the way and your ultimate vision of freedom, you'll want to BE happy now. Be the person now that you want to be, rather than feeling as though you need to wait months, years, or decades out down the road. Why wait? Being that person now allows you to actually enjoy the journey and its plot twists. It allows the journey to unfold more vividly than if you were just waiting until all the external circumstances were present to feel freedom. Look at what your vision is of the financially independent version of you. What kind of person is that? Who are they spending their time with? What are they doing for fun? What are they doing to occupy their time? For example, if you declared that once you reached the Commander or Captain level that then you will learn a language or workout more often, be more disciplined, take more walks—how can you be the person who does that right now, regardless of your current Journeyer level? Maybe the amount of time you can spend actually doing these things will change once you have more autonomy over your time, but you can begin to embody that person now by taking one walk a week, or learning a language by taking out a book from the local library or finding a free video, app or podcast that helps you begin at the basics. Maybe you begin to set aside 15 minutes a week to reach out to call or text your friends and family. You know, the same friends and family you say you will spend more time with once you are Financially Independent but may have not spoken to in months?

Examples of Applying the Be-Do-Have Model to Your Financial Independence Journey

The counterproductive version of the Be-Do-Have model is the Do-Have-Be model, which often prevents you from starting because without believing that you are the kind of person or *the* person to actually have the goal you want, you self-sabotage your progress. Here are some examples that contrast these two models.

The Have (Goal): To Become Credit Card Debt-Free

Do-Have-Be (old way)
You get straight to working on paying off debt; maybe you work more hours for more money and put it toward your credit cards but the amount doesn't feel like it's going down as fast as you like, you still have some of the habits and mindset that got you into debt in the first place, so while you're putting extra money toward your credit cards, you also are

adding to the debt here and there. Be: eventually you become Credit Card Debt–Free.

Be-Do-Have (new way)
Before you get to strategizing about how you will pay off the debt faster you self-reflect on what got you in credit card debt in the first place. You realize that you have a hard time saying no to invites out with friends and overspend when you have your credit card on you and go in the store. You become more disciplined in your use of the credit card and set up systems that help you take your time before saying yes to invites or purchases (a budget, giving yourself space before buying). You then get to work on finding room in the budget you have created. You become Credit Card Debt–Free faster by addressing your mindset and habits first vs. the old model.

The Have (Goal): To Have $100,000 Invested

Do-Have-Be (old way)
You want to invest money but feel discouraged from your goal because it's so far away. You don't believe you can do it so you don't start.

Be-Do-Have (new way)
You know you have a lot of work to do, but you know everyone starts from somewhere. You become more knowledgeable on investing by dedicating some time to listening to personal finance podcasts and reading books on the subject. You may not have a lot of extra money to invest right now, but you know that every little bit counts so you start and open up a Roth IRA and begin investing $100 a month.

OBSTACLES AND OPPORTUNITIES: THE BIOSPHERE 2 EXPERIMENT

The Biosphere 2 experiment in Oracle, Arizona, is the biggest enclosed scientific research facility and project. It was originally meant to demonstrate the viability of closed ecological systems to support and maintain human life in outer space as a substitute for Earth's biosphere. In essence, it was a mini planet with vegetation, including trees, which grew in Biosphere 2 faster than those in a typical environment. Something else happened to them too—they almost always fell down before reaching maturity because of the lack of wind within Biosphere 2. It was found out that the wind was essential to helping a tree grow stronger to handle its own weight. When trees are exposed to wind as they mature, their stress wood, which allows them to support themselves and absorb proper nutrients, becomes stronger. Without the wind, the Biosphere stress wood became deficient and did not allow the tree to reach its full potential, even if it grew faster.

This analogy can be applied to your journey. The wind can be seen as the friction or problems that come along as we are on our path. Whether it's an unexpected emergency, job loss, or the fact that you didn't gain a strong financial foundation from your parents, the circumstances that make you grow slower are in fact conditions that help you grow stronger. Think about what in your life was a lesson or obstacle that you've overcome and you can see how it helped you in the next endeavor or phase of your life. What are you currently going through that feels hard or is an obstacle and how might that help you overcome challenges in the future?

GRATITUDE AND RECOGNIZING PRIVILEGE

It's important to practice gratitude for the things you already have and the progress you've already made so far. No matter where you are on your journey and the stage you're in there is something to be grateful for. Even the things you may find difficult or annoying are things that someone else may be lacking or wishing for. For instance, while you may groan at paying your electricity bill, it's providing you with comfort and light that others without access to electricity or a home of their own would long for. Additionally, even those who appear to have it all, like a happy millionaire with a large house, may still miss the simplicity of a smaller home with fewer expenses.

Many of us have caught ourselves saying "I have to" when faced with daily tasks or responsibilities. However, this language can be indicative of a negative perspective, creating a sense of obligation rather than an opportunity for growth and fulfillment. By shifting your mindset to "I get to," you can cultivate gratitude for the things you have and a positive attitude toward the things you do. In this way, you can begin to appreciate your current circumstances and turn everyday tasks into meaningful experiences.

How can you look at where you are now and turn your "I have to" into "I get to"? For example, instead of saying "I have to," say, "I get to." "I have to go to work" becomes "I get to go to work." "I have to pay my bills" becomes "I get to pay my bills." Think of some of the things that you complain about and turn them into things you are thankful for.

RECONCILING INTERNAL MINDSET AND EXTERNAL REALITY

Your external reality includes the facts you have in front of you. This includes the consequences of your own actions, such as taking out excessive student loans, as well as factors outside of your control, like the lack of guidance and information provided by others in your life or at school. Your current external reality may be that you are still in debt and don't have much invested, yet your internal mentality should not be defined by your current situation. You don't have to wait until you reach the stage you want to be in before you adjust your mentality. Just because you are in an Explorer or Cadet stage now doesn't mean you have to be locked into an Explorer or Cadet mindset. What would the Commander or Captain you be thinking or doing in this situation? They would likely take ownership of their role in their circumstances and view the situation as temporary, empowering them to seek out solutions and become the person they are meant to be. This shift in mindset can help them overcome the situation and move forward with determination.

BREAKING OUT OF THE ANT MILL

Thought and behavior death loops are similar to the phenomenon that happens to an ant called the ant mill or death spiral. It happens when some ants lose track of their colony or separate from their foraging party and then follow the ant in front of them in a circle continuously. The ants often end up dying of exhaustion. Following our thoughts and existing mindset can be like that, one thought after another like each ant follows the other round and round. We must find the thought that can break the cycle or we will work ourselves to a mental and emotional death. It's not surprising to find ourselves stuck in a cycle of work and spending, feeling unfulfilled and unaware of alternative paths, if we merely follow or replicate the examples presented to us. However, you have the opportunity to break free from this pattern and discover a new path, the path to FI. You can be the one to chart your own course and explore new possibilities.

HABITS

ASSESSING CURRENT HABITS

What habits are helping you with your goals and which are hindering you? You can track your habits just like you can your expenses to assess which habit you want to stop, start, increase, or decrease. Most of our habits can be tracked as they are actual things we do, such as waking up at a certain time, brushing our teeth, eating breakfast, etc. For one week track how you spend your time and your feelings throughout the day. If you're like me then the thought of this is tedious. Consider this a temporary experiment, not something you'll need to do for the rest of your life, just something you're doing now to get a clear grasp of how you spend your time and to pick up on habits you may or may not know you are doing. You can track your time in twenty-minute increments. Note when you wake up, the first thing that you do, when you eat, start working, or the activities you do. The purpose here is to get a sense of any patterns and behaviors you have or don't have. We often think we don't have enough time to implement the changes we want to see in our lives. Just like seeing where our expenses are going through creating and keeping a budget, managing our time and understanding clearly where we are spending it and what we are doing with it can create opportunities to correct negative habits and build new positive ones. However, unlike money which can be limitless, our time and how much we get of it while we are on this earth, is finite.

If you're honest with yourself, you probably already know some of your counterproductive money habits that you need to change without even writing them down. For example, maybe you know that you have a habit of online shopping when you're bored, which causes you to spend money on things you don't really need.

There are some habits that are counterproductive to your financial journey that may not be as obvious to you. We will call those your ripple-effect money habits.

The difference between direct money habits and ripple-effect money habits are that direct money habits are things that you do that directly impact your finances. Ripple-effect habits are the habits that don't directly seem correlated with your money, but which set off a chain of negative or positive actions.

Examples of Direct Positive Money Habits

- Creating a monthly budget
- Reconciling budget on a consistent basis throughout the month
- Packing your own lunch

- Eating breakfast at home
- Making coffee at home
- Reading specific money book
- Listening to money podcasts

Examples of Ripple-Effect Positive Money Habits

- Getting a good night's rest
- Listening to self-development or inspirational podcasts
- Reading self-development or inspirational books
- Exercising or physical activity

EXAMPLE OF A RIPPLE-EFFECT POSITIVE MONEY HABIT

Getting a good night's rest

Waking up early and feeling refreshed

Eating breakfast at home and packing lunch

Not having to buy breakfast or lunch at work and saving money

EXAMPLE OF A RIPPLE-EFFECT NEGATIVE MONEY HABIT

Going to be late and not getting a good night's rest

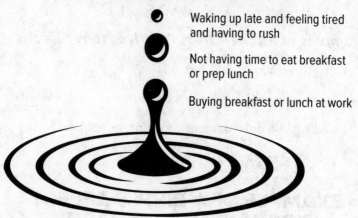

Waking up late and feeling tired and having to rush

Not having time to eat breakfast or prep lunch

Buying breakfast or lunch at work

It's important to at least know the habits you have that are impacting your journey so that you can know if you want to change them.

On the surface, a thought or habit can seem totally unrelated to your finances. But everything you do can impact your money, just as your money impacts everything you do. The way you think about yourself and what's possible for you ripples out—the same way the lack of a routine or healthy habits will impact you.

6

UNCOVERING YOUR DESIRED LIFE GOALS AND DETERMINING YOUR GUACAMOLE LEVEL

While the numbers are important, don't worry—we're getting there. I want you to have a clear sense of your goals—and not just your financial goals like paying off a credit card or buying a house, but your life goals and dreams. What do you want your actual life to look like? Where do you want to live? What do you want to do with your time? Who do you want to spend your time with? These are important questions to ask yourself because you won't know you've reached your destination if you haven't decided what you are aiming for. Your answers to the questions above may change over time but you'll need to have a sense of where your rocket is headed before launching or you'll be aimlessly orbiting or end up at a destination you never intended.

While ending up at a surprise destination or places you never expected can sometimes be a good thing, in order to plot your plan to move from where you are now to your desired Journeyer level, you need to know the end point. Many people are passively living their life, letting things happen to them or giving other people the power to make decisions that will impact their lives. Mapping out your journey is really about empowering yourself to take action and figuring out what you truly want.

If you want to create an FI plan that you enjoy and that reflects your true desires, you'll need to determine your life objectives. I'll give you some exercises that you can complete to help uncover your life goals and then later, I'll introduce the Guacamole Lifestyle Levels, which help you identify your desired standard of living at present and in the future once you achieve FI.

> **Life goals** revolve around the desired experiences you want and the person you aspire to become throughout your lifetime. These objectives may encompass both long-term aspirations that require saving and investments as well as smaller aspirations that can be integrated into daily life through discretionary expenses.

LIFE GOALS

I want to start with identifying your life goals because that's more fun than financial goals. Looking at our goals solely from a financial perspective limits us to seeing only what's feasible in terms of numbers. When we imagine what we want in our lives without considering financial constraints, our mind becomes more imaginative. By incorporating our life goals into our planning, we can explore possibilities in full color, with a sense of vibrancy and excitement. This approach enables us to be more creative in finding ways to achieve both our life goals and financial goals as they work harmoniously together.

First, I'm going to encourage you to spend some time dreaming about *the life you truly want*—not the life society says you should have. We have so much pressure from the outside world—society, friends, and family—who all tell us what they think we should have.

Who did you want to be before the world told you who you should become? You may be thinking, *Well how do I know what I really want if I've been conditioned to listen to outside influences for years?* Part of learning about what you truly want is embracing your why (more on your why—and your why not—later in this chapter). For instance, maybe you're concerned because you think you want something for a superficial reason. I think we should establish that it is okay to want things for superficial reasons. Almost everything we want or have is because we think having it will make us feel better or make others view us in a more favorable way. Perhaps you love to cook and want a fancy, restaurant-caliber home kitchen. Or maybe you want to roll up to the family reunion in a flashy new car. Recognizing and admitting your motivations is an important part of the process.

Don't trick or lie to yourself about the why behind your desires—take ownership. We have enough messaging from the media and society trying to influence and steer us to participate in capitalism by using false claims and advertising. There's no need for you to do that to yourself. Being honest with yourself will allow you to identify your life and financial goals and give you perspective on how to prioritize your goals.

A life goal or target can be more about where you want to live or the places you want to vacation and includes what your day-to-day life looks like. For example, maybe you want to move to an island one day permanently or do slow travel around the world for a few years. You envision a daily life of waking up to the sound of the ocean, where most of your day is spent writing or working on a special project.

Here are a few specific examples of life goals:

- I want to travel the world for two months.

- I want to live near a beach.

- I want a flexible work situation where I can work remotely.

- I want to have more time to exercise.

- I want to write a book.

TOOLS TO IDENTIFY YOUR LIFE GOALS

Dream a (Not So) Little Dream

One way to discover what you want is to think back to your hopes and dreams as a child or teenager. Was there somewhere you dreamed about going, or did you have an interest or talent that you enjoyed? What did you want to be when you grew up before the adults in your life told you it wasn't realistic or possible? While we can outgrow our childhood or teenage desires, many times those innocent and unfiltered dreams can act as a compass to figure out what we truly want.

When I was younger, I thought I'd be a writer or lawyer because of my love for reading and talking. I had no problem advocating for myself, although the older folks in my family may have called it talking back. I was even awarded a writing award in elementary school and remember a time where I was obsessed with books like Sister Souljah's *The Coldest Winter Ever* and began writing my own soon-to-be-classic urban coming-of-age stories. I loved writing poetry and expressing myself. Some of my friends even nicknamed me "Logic" because of my ability to see reason and share different points of views on the same topic. As for financial goals, I wanted to have what I thought was a lot of money at the time: a million dollars to be exact. I also enjoyed having my freedom and never understood the need for pointless rules or people telling me what to do.

When I think back on who I was as a child and what I enjoyed doing, it makes sense that for most of my twenties I felt off because I'd forgotten about some of the things that made me happy. Even though I'd tried entrepreneurial things throughout college and in my twenties like starting the magazine *Empress*, investing in vending machines, and getting my real estate salesperson license, once those things failed to make money or become a success, I resigned myself to working a nine-to-five for the rest of my life. How else was I going to pay for my living expenses? When I became an adult with adult bills, I thought I had to let my childish dreams die out. I stopped reading and writing as much and slowly gave up my dreams of being rich and quitting my corporate job.

It was through remembering who I was and what I enjoyed doing that I found my way to more freedom. I started following my interests and the hyperlinks in my life I mentioned in the introduction that unfolded into the life I have now.

Reflecting on what made you happy or excited before you were an adult is one way to start getting to the root of what you want out of life. Another way is to think about what matters to you today. If something in your life was taken away from you—a simple pleasure like going out to eat, taking vacations, or driving a nice car—how would that make you feel? Would you miss that thing if you didn't have it or couldn't do it for a year? If not, then that's probably not an essential part of your dream life. You can apply this thought process to your job, personal relationships, or even where you live. For example, if your boss called you into their office and fired you or your partner told you they wanted to call it quits, apart from a possible wounded ego and wounded heart, would you feel relieved? If so, then you know that the job or relationship isn't what you truly want.

George Kinder's Three Questions

George Kinder, a financial planner, author, and founder of the Kinder Institute of Life Planning, is considered a pioneer in the field of financial life planning. Kinder emphasizes the importance of aligning your financial goals with your values, passions, and life goals. To create a financial plan for yourself is to understand what your overall life plan is. This is how you find out what motivates you and what your priorities are.

These three scenarios and accompanying questions foster self-examination as you dive deeper and deeper to figure out your true inner workings:

1. I want you to imagine that you are financially secure, that you have enough money to take care of your needs,

now and in the future. The question is…how would you live your life? Would you change anything? Let yourself go. Don't hold back on your dreams.

2. You are back in your current financial situation. Your doctor tells you that you have five to ten years to live, and you will feel fine up until the end. Would you change your life and, if so, how would you change it?

3. Imagine that your doctor tells you that you have just one day to live. You look back on your life and ask what did you fail to experience, who is the person that you did *not* become, and what did you neglect to do?

"Dream Life" Exercise

To help you further figure out what you want from your life, I want to share with you an exercise that blew me away when I first heard it, Debbie Millman's "Ten-Year Plan for a Remarkable Life." Millman is an American author and educator who has been recognized as one of the most influential designers in the world. Millman attended a course at the School of Visual Arts in 2005, taught by renowned designer Milton Glaser. One of the exercises he assigned in the class was to write an essay that envisioned one's life five years down the line, including everything they desired and would do if they had no fear of failure. Millman eventually began teaching it to her students and turned it into a ten-year exercise.

Here's how the Ten-Year Plan works: Pick a day ten years from now and describe every detail of it. The exercise is meant for you to design your future life. Millman says that not only has everything in her own Ten-Year Plan come true, but hundreds of her students also have had their Ten-Year Plans come to fruition.

While you may have heard of similar exercises like this before, Millman explains it in such an eloquent way that you can't help but feel inspired and ready to take action. In the interview, she invites listeners to imagine their lives. She asks questions about what their lives are like, where and with whom they're living, and what their clothes, furniture and pets like. She prompts listeners to think about their families and careers, to imagine what excites them. She encourages them to picture every detail of what a day might look like in that life, and then to dream about it, write it down, and read it once a year—then see what happens.

The idea is that the more specific and the more in depth you describe your life in ten years, the more likely it will be to come true. This is due to what psychologists refer to as prospection, the evaluation of possible futures and mental time travel, the capacity to imagine possible scenarios in the future. Once you have a future vision, you're more likely to adjust your current actions and make better decisions to help you accomplish that vision. Studies also show that the greater connection you feel between who you are today, your nearer self, and who you will be twenty to thirty years from now, your remote self, the more you're willing to wait for a larger reward and delay gratification.

Money by itself will not make you happy or content—it's simply just a tool to get what you want out of life. If that weren't the case, the Ten-Year Plan instructions would simply be "Write down how much money you want to have in your bank account in ten years." Just writing down a number won't get you to where you want to be. While it's important to have specific financial goals (we'll get to that later), it's equally important to design a life you truly want to live.

Your perfect life won't happen because you have money—you will have money because you have created a perfect life.

Know Your Why—And Your Why Not

"Figuring Out Your Why" is often used as a prompt or exercise to identify the motivation behind your goals. I'd argue that knowing your Why Not is equally important to determining how intensely you want to reach your goals and what those goals should actually be.

My Why is my kids. With each pregnancy and child I felt this undeniable force within me to pursue a life of flexibility and freedom. It was that excruciating commute while I was heavily pregnant with my first son, Zach, that pushed me to search for an escape from the rat race and led me to discover the FIRE movement. It was my second child, Luke, that encouraged me to officially start the blog *Journey to Launch* to document my own journey to financial independence. Becoming pregnant with my third child, my daughter, Blake, pushed me further into action. Knowing I was pregnant and when I was going to give birth provided me with the immovable deadline of when I wanted to quit my job. I was scheduled to give birth in May, so I'd use my maternity leave and then give them notice that I would not be returning. Since everyone was expecting me to be out for four months, I was able to train my colleagues to pick up my responsibilities.

The last day in the office, I packed my things to say goodbye, but they didn't know it would be goodbye for good. My desk was clear, my responsibilities had all been given to other people, and I gave my last hugs to everyone. It felt bittersweet because I knew I wouldn't see them again. Was I making the right decision? Would they need me?

Weeks before my maternity leave was scheduled to end, I called my boss from the bathroom floor nervous and holding my breath as I informed him I wouldn't be returning. He didn't seem that surprised and offered me his well-wishes on my next adventure.

The moment had arrived, I was setting out on the next step of my path to becoming a full-time entrepreneur. Even though I hadn't achieved financial independence yet, I had reached a new level, the Commander phase, where I had greater control over my time and the way I earned a living. Despite having doubts, when I gazed at my three children, I was certain that I was headed in the right direction.

Is your goal to earn more? Ask yourself why. Is it so you can live an upgraded lifestyle? So you can invest more money and have more financial security? So you can buy your dream car? The why or reason behind wanting to accomplish your goal should be the main focus. When we set goals without knowing why, we can end up lost, or not understanding what we're really pursuing. How do you know if you've reached your "enough point" of earning more or spending less if you don't have a reason behind it? Especially if you find yourself trading your time for money, and you have to work more hours or more years to earn more money, you may find yourself trying to fill an insatiable void.

My kids are not only my Why but also my Why Not.

Looking back, my motivation to find financial independence, start the journey, and eventually quit my job all came because I knew what I would not tolerate because of them. For instance, I refused to put up with a two- to three-hour commute for the rest of my life, which would deprive me of valuable time with my kids or to work in a job that made me unhappy and less present. Because of my kids, I find empowerment in saying no to things that don't align with my values or that will take up too much time. Knowing my Why Not helps me narrow down the goals I want to pursue and prioritize what truly matters.

The Where matters more than you think. Where you want to live and the setting of your life matters more than others make it out to be. Sometimes you'll hear people say, "It doesn't matter where you are or where you live—you can be happy anywhere," or "Don't let outside circumstances dictate how you feel." But the setting of the story in which your life takes place—where you wake up, the weather, the smell, the way the room looks—matter to your general well-being. For example, moving to an LCOL (low cost of living) area from an HCOL (high cost of living) area can save you a lot of money and is one of the biggest changes you can make that impacts your budget and the length of time it takes you to reach your money goals. But if you love the city you are in—HCOL be damned, or if you have support through family and friends there that you're not willing to leave behind for the sake of saving money—then you have to acknowledge that. It's not that you can't make yourself happy somewhere else; it just doesn't appeal to you. If you're unwilling to give up your Where, you'll need to look at your budget to find areas to either cut back on (expenses) or expand on (income) to help you reach your financial goals.

GUACAMOLE LIFESTYLE LEVELS

When I first got into the idea of becoming financially independent, my life became a lot *smaller*. I drank the frugality Kool-Aid. I tried to spend as little as possible. I stopped buying clothes. I canceled subscriptions left and right. I negotiated every bill and aggressively paid off my debt with the extra cash I had created.

But then…I realized that I wanted to order guacamole.

So simple. Yet so annoying.

I live in Brooklyn, and one of my favorite things to do is go out with my friends for Tex-Mex. Even when I was strictly sticking to a budget and watching my spending, I allowed myself the splurge of a margarita every now and then. But the guacamole woke me up to the difference between financial independence and financial freedom. When I was honest with myself, I acknowledged that I wanted to order the guacamole more than save $12 to achieve financial independence a little bit sooner in the future.

Like a lot of people, I want to enjoy my life now. I want more than the no-frills lifestyle many personal finance experts and the entire FIRE community talk about. I want to order guacamole and go on family vacations multiple times a year and have the option to get my hair done at a fancy salon.

And I can have those things, because I have learned the difference between achieving financial independence and financial freedom. Remember, you can have financial freedom while on your journey to financial independence. In other words, you can have your guacamole *and* secure your financial future too.

Oftentimes when you set your lifestyle and money goals, you'll need to make "in the meantime" adjustments to achieve your goals. I'm not going to tell you that sacrifices won't be made. But they don't have to be painful, and you don't have to feel miserable. You can negotiate with yourself about what you will delay or deny yourself. You will be uncomfortable at times, but that's part of the journey. There is a difference between a discomfort that you think will last a lifetime and feels never-ending vs. discomfort and sacrifice that you know is temporary. The sacrifices you will need to make now to secure your financial future—which will allow you to have all the options in the world—will be worth it. And dare I say they might even begin to feel good? For example, challenging yourself to find more money to invest from your budget may involve cutting back on going out to eat, but in the interim, you may find creative ways to prepare your own food and discover a love for cooking you never knew you had.

Your life goals will have a financial component to them, meaning they will cost money to achieve. Although these two types of goals are different, they go hand in hand. In order to help you identify your desired level of lifestyle and spending and how it compares to the way you live and spend now, I've come up with something called Guacamole levels or Guac levels for short. (Can you tell how much I love guacamole? If you hate guacamole, feel free to replace it with your favorite treat or thing.)

The Guac levels go from 1 to 5, 1 being the least amount of fanciness and 5 being the highest level of indulgence. By asking a question about a simple lifestyle choice—Do you order the guacamole or not?—you can determine what lifestyle level of financial freedom you want.

As I explain the Guac levels, I want you to reflect on your current level and which level you aim to achieve on your FI journey.

THE GUAC LEVELS

GUAC LEVEL 1 is characterized by having no extras. Your focus is on FI, and you prioritize your baseline and mandatory expenses—housing, transportation, and groceries—to survive. You live a traditionally frugal lifestyle and rarely indulge in anything beyond your basic needs.

GUAC LEVEL 2 has occasional extras. You may indulge in something like eating out or ordering guacamole, but only on special occasions or when a good discount is available. Extras like these are considered significant expenses, and you would not indulge in them regularly.

GUAC LEVEL 3 is where you indulge in extras like eating out or ordering guacamole more frequently because you enjoy them and consider them a source of luxury in your life. You have a designated budget to cover such expenses, and they are a regular part of your routine.

GUAC LEVEL 4 is where you can have extras whenever you want, regardless of the price. You are willing to pay a premium for high-quality luxury experiences, including expensive appetizers like guacamole. Money is not a significant barrier for you, and you can indulge in extras regularly without being too concerned with fitting them into your budget. You would pay $19 for fresh guacamole made with organic ingredients at the table just like you would pay for first-class flights.

GUAC LEVEL 5 is the ultimate level of luxury, where you have your own chef in-house to make authentic guacamole whenever you want, in addition to ordering it whenever and wherever you go out. At this level, you can indulge in anything you desire, including daily tubs of guacamole. You are a total baller and probably own a private jet. You are at the top of the financial ladder and have the ability to enjoy life's pleasures without any restrictions.

Frugal				Extravagant
GUAC LEVEL 1	GUAC LEVEL 2	GUAC LEVEL 3	GUAC LEVEL 4	GUAC LEVEL 5
Lower FI # needed				Higher FI # needed

So what option appeals to you? I choose option #4.

While I don't require every luxurious item available, I do have a soft spot for guacamole, and more than that, I value the flexibility and freedom to choose how I use my money. Admittedly, it's possible to reach my FI goals faster by eliminating extras like appetizers. However, I find it less appealing and practical to live that way and prefer enjoying my life today. Every decision comes with trade-offs, which is the opportunity cost of relinquishing one desire to attain another.

It's important to understand why you have chosen your desired Guac level and to be honest with yourself about your motivations. Ask yourself these questions:

1. Are you currently living a Guac level 1 lifestyle with the intention of being able to live a Guac level 3 in the future? Are you comfortable with sacrificing everyday indulgences now to achieve this goal later?

2. Do you prefer living a simple lifestyle at Guac level 1 or 2 and plan to maintain that same level in the future when you reach FI?

3. What Guac level can you realistically live at now while working toward an FI that aligns with the Guac level you want to maintain once you reach FI? This way, you won't feel like you're sacrificing your current quality of life to achieve your financial goals. For instance, if you aspire to live at Guac level 3, you may choose to live at that level while on the path to FI and continue that lifestyle once you reach it.

You can be a Guac level 1 or 2 in some areas of your life

because they are not as important to you to spend on and a Guac 3 or 4 level in other areas because you value them. For example, I'm more of Guac level 2 on clothes but more of a Guac level 3 or 4 on vacations and experiences. Overall I'd place my total Guac level at 4. Even if I don't spend highly in some areas now, I want to reserve the right to spend more in the areas when I feel I like it.

You may currently be living a Guac level but not by choice. You don't enjoy it and want more out of life and to be able to spend more money without feeling restricted. Or you may actually like this level and come to an agreement with yourself that you're willing to give up the Guac for achieving your goals faster.

As I shared in the introduction, when I first learned about the FIRE movement, I was stuck in a horrible commute and disliked my job. I desperately wanted to get out as fast as possible. I knew that to reach the aggressive FIRE goal I set for myself to quit my job at forty so that I didn't have to work again, my husband and I would need to live a modest Guac level 2. I also thought that to reach my calculated FI number, we'd have to live that modest Guac level 2 lifestyle after I quit my job and was "retired." To make the numbers work, we cut back on going out to eat and going on vacations. At the time, we were fine with that. It was worth it to cut back on these extras to reach our big, audacious goals.

But as we started saving and investing more and as our family started to grow, I realized that I didn't want to live the Guac level 2 lifestyle forever. I wanted to go out to eat more, take nice vacations, fly first-class and put my kids in activities without worrying about every dollar spent. Guac level 2 now and in the future felt too restrictive based on our lifestyle desires and goals. So we started making more room for the splurges and cut back on investing. I also made a big decision to quit my job.

Remember Purple, mentioned in Chapter 1? She made the decision to retire early and enjoy a life of leisure instead of continuing to work in her corporate job until retirement age. Despite earning more money, she kept her expenses low while working so that she could achieve her goal of retiring by the age of thirty. As a result of her efforts, her net worth increased from $5,000 to over $500,000 in nine years. While working, she spent around $20,000 annually and now spends about the same amount in retirement. However, she does not feel that she is sacrificing luxury, and in fact, she believes she is able to indulge in the areas that matter most to her. In the two years following her early retirement, she was able to travel to multiple states and even internationally, all while maintaining her spending at around $20,000. By not being restricted by a job, she is able to travel and take advantage of lower costs of living in different parts of the world. Due to her flexible schedule, she has greater options allowing her to get discounted flights and accommodations, but can still maintain a level of quality travel. While her overall spending is more in line with the lower Guac level range, she can still indulge in the same experiences as someone who spends more at Guac 3 or 4 level. While some may not find Purple's spending to be sufficient for their lifestyle needs, she is content and comfortable with her relatively low spending and has the option to spend more money if she wants.

As someone who thought choosing a Guac level 2 lifestyle was something I could enjoy and live with for the rest of my life, I had to be real with myself and what I wanted. A Guac level 2 lifestyle just doesn't work for me, and since I want to live a Guac Level 4 in retirement and while on the path to FI, I recognize that I'll need to make and have more money in the bank and in my investment accounts to support the lifestyle I desire—and that I'll probably work longer or need to make a lot more money than my frugal counterparts. To be clear, no option or level is wrong. This is all about what *you* want and what *you* are willing to sacrifice (or not sacrifice) as you embark on this journey.

The Guac level of freedom you currently have vs. what you're working toward as a sustained lifestyle may be different. You may have to operate on Guac level 1 or 2 for a few months or few years so that you can live at Guac level 3, 4, or 5 indefinitely. Oftentimes, getting out of debt or kick-starting your investments takes time. The real magic happens when you are actually living the desired Guac lifestyle you want and aspire to have in FI and retirement. You've reached a level that feels good and can be sustained. There are still opportunity costs associated with your decisions and you may not be able to have everything at the same time, but you are content with your life.

Only you can determine what you truly want from your life, as you make decisions based on what you know now—or what's best for you at any point in time. With more experience, trial and error, and the tools in this book, I hope to help you determine what your flexible—and enjoyable!—journey to financial independence looks like.

7

SETTING FINANCIAL GOALS

Financial goals are about the specific money goals you want to achieve related to saving, investing, paying off debt, or purchasing something.

Your financial goals will generally fall under one of five categories: Income, Spending, Saving, Investing, and Debt Payoff. The Income and Spending goals are the lead goals or domino goals and the Saving, Investing, and Debt Payoff Goals are your gap goals, the goals you can accomplish with the gap we talked about in the FI formula. Typically if you want to save, invest, or pay off debt, you'll need to find room in your budget by first accomplishing your income and spending goals. Knock those two dominos down and the others will fall because accomplishing those goals allows you to reach the remaining three goals:

FIVE FINANCIAL GOALS

LEAD OR DOMINO GOALS		
GOAL TYPE	**DESCRIPTION**	**EXAMPLES**
1. Income	A financial goal tied to how much you make	• I want to earn $1,000 more a month or I want a salary of $100,000. • I want to make $30,000 more in three years.
2. Spending	A financial goal tied to how much you want to spend, usually cutting back in an area	• I want to spend $200 a month on going out to eat instead of the $500 I'm currently spending.

Earning more and/or spending less will generate
the money needed to reach your other three goals.

GAP GOALS		
GOAL TYPE	**DESCRIPTION**	**EXAMPLES**
3. Saving	A financial goal tied to saving for something specific	• I want to save $5,000 in my emergency fund. • I want to save up a $20,000 FU fund in two years. • I want to save up a down payment of $25,000 for a house in four years. • You can also add in your lifestyle goals here—e.g., I want to save $2,000 for a trip.
4. Debt Payoff	A financial goal tied to paying off debt	• I want to pay off $5,000 of credit card debt. • I want to pay off $30,000 in credit card debt in five years.
5. Investing	A financial goal tied to investing	• I want to consistently invest $500 a month. • I want to invest at least $200 a month.

CATEGORIZING AND PRIORITIZING YOUR GOALS

It's time to organize your goals in a way that gives you clarity on which ones you want to tackle first. Goals can be sorted into multiple categories that sometimes overlap. For example, a life goal of traveling the world does have a financial goal component to it—how else could you afford the trip? Or you have goals that feel equally important and pressing, like getting out of debt and buying your first home. How do you know what to prioritize?

The way you first think about and break out your goals matters. Most people either think about their goals according to a finite number or are too vague with their goals. You can have financial goals based on a number or specific number outcome. You can also have life goals that are not associated with numbers but are more of a general accomplishment, feeling, or thing. These goals can then be broken out by when you want to accomplish them, within three different time frames:

- Immediate/short-term—goals you want to accomplish within one year

- Mid-term—goals you want to accomplish in one to five years

- Long-term—goals you want to accomplish in five plus years

Once you start to calculate the cost associated with each goal, you may need to adjust your time frame to be more realistic based on your circumstances and how much money you can apply toward that goal. Maybe at the start of this process you put down that you want to be credit card debt-free within one year, but after running the numbers you assess that it will take you three years to reach your goal. In this initial run of planning your goals, you will use the information you have today to make your best guess based on what you currently know. You can always refine your list and the specifics as you gather more information.

One of the complicated things with not just goal setting but actually following through on completing your goals is to balance between your future desires and the responsible goals you feel you need to set for yourself (e.g., I want to invest a majority of my income for the future me) vs. the things you want now (I want to take that expensive trip to Saint Lucia this summer). Oftentimes the life goals list will be the "fun list" and the financial goals list will be the responsible "should-do" list. However, both lists matter because when you understand how they interact—part enjoying the now and part being responsible for the future—you can begin to balance between the two.

Get the most updated version of these resources and other tools via your complimentary Your Journey to Financial Freedom Toolkit at www.yourjourneytofinancialfreedom.com.

Step 1: Do a goal dump.
Write out a list of all your financial and lifestyle goals. Don't censor yourself or try to make the goals perfect, just dump it all out.

Step 2: Organize goals by time frame.
Write all immediate and short-term goals together in one

column, mid-term goals in another column, and long-term goals in another column.

Step 3: Prioritize goals by importance.
Prioritize your goals by time frame in order of importance. What would you like to accomplish first?

Step 4: Calculate how much each goal costs.
Figure out how much is needed to accomplish or experience that goal. To determine the varying range of how much you'd need to save, use the Guac levels. For example, if you wanted to travel the world on a bare-bones Guac 1-2 level, how much would that cost? Which level feels both doable and gratifying? Pick a total amount for now and work backward to figure out how much you need to save monthly to achieve that goal by the desired time frame. Divide the total cost of the goal by the number of years or months in which you want it to be accomplished. For example: if you set a goal of saving $10,000 in two years to take a family vacation, it would be $10,000 / 24 months = $416 a month (you'd need to save $416 a month to achieve that goal in two years).

Keep this list and numbers handy so that you can incorporate your most important goals into your ongoing budget.

GOAL FUEL

Now that you have identified your goals, it's time to figure out how you will accomplish them. This is where "Goal Fuel" comes in. As you work toward a specific goal, Goal Fuel, which refers to the things you will specifically work on, will give you the fuel you need to accomplish them. (Notice that these are a part of the FI formula.)

The four Goal Fuels are:

- Mindset Goal Fuel: How can you improve your mindset around this goal?

- Habit Goal Fuel: What habits can you alter to help you achieve this goal?

- Income Goal Fuel: How can you increase your income to achieve this goal?

- Expenses Goal Fuel: What can you cut back on or eliminate from your expenses to achieve this goal? (And in some cases, how can you spend/invest in a way that helps you achieve this goal?)

You don't have to work on all four components at once, but being intentional about which ones you are actively working on will give you better chances of achieving that goal. For example, let's say you set a goal to pay off $5,000 of credit card debt in three years. Here is how you use Goal Fuel to help you accomplish that.

Mindset Goal Fuel: Working to view your past decisions as lessons instead of mistakes. This helps you give yourself grace and not to bash yourself for past financial decisions, which allows you to have a more positive view of yourself and be more optimistic about your financial future.

Habit Goal Fuel: You no longer take your credit card with you to Target. You purchase with a specific list and pay with cash, which helps you eliminate overspending.

Income Goal Fuel: You increase your income by negotiating a higher salary at your job over the next year and pick up a side hustle to bring in additional income that you will use to pay off debt.

Expenses Goal Fuel: You will cancel cable and use the money saved to go toward your credit card payment.

IT'S OKAY TO CHANGE YOUR MIND

What financial freedom means to you isn't what it means to me. And what it means to you now, won't necessarily be the same years, months, or maybe even weeks from now. The definition of financial freedom evolves as our goals change and our priorities shift. There was a time in my life when I wanted a lot of fancy stuff—a beautiful home with a lot of bedrooms for my kids, a nice car for my husband, and a luxurious annual vacation with my entire family. And that was fine until my priorities shifted. In fact, when I first started my journey, I decreased my goals and the type of life I wanted to live. Now I'm more in a middle ground where I still want a nice house but it doesn't have to have lots of bedrooms. And while we are taking nicer vacations and spending to upgrade our current home, at the moment I'm not willing to work harder or more to achieve that lifestyle.

True freedom is having the confidence to change your mind and try something different. After all, the whole point of having money is so that you can ENJOY IT. Most people think that the journey to financial freedom means deprivation. However, there's a difference between deprivation and sacrifice. Deprivation focuses on what you're losing: *I can't have this today, tomorrow, or the day after.* In contrast, sacrifice focuses on what you're gaining: *I can't have this today, but be-*

cause of that, I can have this tomorrow. Sacrificing keeps you focused on the greater reward and purpose.

For our ten-year wedding anniversary my husband and I took our most expensive vacation to date. We went to a world-renowned resort in Saint Lucia, famous for its unique architecture. Each room has an open fourth wall with a view of the majestic Piton mountains and a pool.

I never would have spent my money on a vacation like that when I was in my twenties. I wasn't into quality vacations the way I am now. Back then I'd look for the cheapest hotel and cheapest airline, and if it were a girls' trip, we'd fit as many of us in the room as possible. On a girls' trip to South Beach, my friends and I sat down in the sweltering sun on the beach and refused to pay the $10 for an umbrella and chair. So we were all uncomfortable and hot and eventually got sunburned. We had the money, but for some reason we thought it wasn't worth $10 to alleviate the discomfort. Today, I will pay for comfort and luxury.

The reason for the shift in my behavior is because my definition of freedom has changed. And so has my financial situation. When I went on the trip to Saint Lucia, I had already paid off my debt and bought a home. Back then, I was content with a Guacamole 2 lifestyle and didn't see the value in an expensive hotel room. It was all about spending the least amount of money while still having fun. Freedom meant saving, scrimping, and living a more frugal lifestyle so that I could reach my financial goals by any means possible. Now, freedom means enjoying my life and having the ability to splurge every now and then. My taste and preferences evolved as I got older and the ability to focus on my life goals also has expanded because I moved up in Journeyer levels. I want to afford myself more than just the basic comforts of life which means ordering the expensive guacamole when I feel like it and paying for a beach chair and umbrella while on vacation.

GOALPOSTS AND SETTING GOAL MINIMUMS & MAXIMUMS

Consider looking at your goals as a series of goalposts as opposed to a fixed goal in the end zone. We all know the feeling of setting a goal and accomplishing it, then feeling like it's not enough and having to set another goal. It can feel like we are on a never-ending journey. We succeed at reaching what we thought would be one delicious goal and yet the hunger still exists. This is a shared human experience and nothing to feel bad about. This normal phenomenon is also known as the hedonic treadmill, which describes the tendency for humans to strive for one pleasure after another. The idea is that when you achieve or get something, it then becomes the baseline. Then you're no longer as stimulated by or interested in the goal you've just achieved, so you want something else. The cycle can be related to our desire to want more material items or money. For example, once we get our dream car we enjoy it for a bit, but then the newness rubs off and we set our sights on a new dream car.

This same experience can happen with our money goals. We say we want to save $5,000 and when we achieve that, we decide that saving $10,000 would be better. Or maybe we set our salary goal at $90,000 but when we get there we think, *Hey, I deserve $125,000.* Adjusting your goals as you reach them is completely fine—and there's nothing wrong with wanting more. But in planning out your future goals you should be mindful about how your perspective may change once you reach them. Plus, let's not forget about the impact of inflation and unforeseen circumstances that may arise, which could result in the need for a higher amount of money or a change in goals.

I like to look at the minimum amount of money needed to reach a financial or lifestyle goal and the maximum amount of money needed to reach that same financial or lifestyle goal. The minimum goal amount sets a baseline for what will make you happy even if you can't have it at the top level or luxury that you want. Looking at it this way, you're always in the position to win because your minimum goals are not a compromise of your happiness and what you want to achieve. If nothing else happens beyond that, I've already won. If something else does happen, I reach my "pie in the sky" goal and win some more. Understanding how to set and use goalposts and work with minimums and maximums will be important as you think about what your financial independence journey looks like.

For example, let's consider the following goals broken down on a range of minimum and maximum amounts needed to reach or experience that goal. Remember the minimum amount you assign is still something you'd be happy with.

Taking two months to travel:
- minimum: bare-bones travel budget $5,000; maximum: more luxurious travel budget $15,000

Buying a house:
- minimum: condo or smaller house $250,000; maximum: bigger house, $425,000

SETTING AND BALANCING FINANCIAL GOALS AND LIFE GOALS BY JOURNEYER LEVELS

Your life goals don't need to be altered because you are at a beginning Journeyer level. Your life goals can be big as you want, whether you are in debt or currently finding your financial footing. The life goals you are actively working toward can change by Journeyer level, but you deserve whatever life goals you want. Remember that your life goals can be part long-term goals you want to accomplish and part of how you spend today via your discretionary expenses.

For every financial goal you are actively working toward, you should also pick a life goal to work toward or can spend on today. This helps balance your energy between doing the responsible thing for a fruitful future and the more enjoyable things you want to do now. For example, if you are in the Cadet stage, paying off your credit card debt will be your primary mission, but you can still work to experience your life goals at the same time by budgeting in advance for spa treatments and slowly saving toward your dream vacation in the future.

As you progress in the Journeyer stages, how much you spend
or resources you put into financial vs lifestyle goals change.
Earlier stages, you put more resources/money into financial goals, etc.

8

CREATING YOUR
FINANCIAL INDEPENDENCE PLAN

Now that we've covered what FI is and the stages you need to go through to reach it, along with identifying how the components of the FI formula work, it's time to get started on creating your own FI plan. This is my favorite part of the process. This is where you get to apply your actual numbers and can begin to map out how long it will take you. I remember what it was like when I first saw my real numbers and mapped out different FI scenarios. Using my Excel skills that I picked up from work, I began to create what would become what I call the "Fire Calc" spreadsheet, a spreadsheet that allowed me to calculate how much I needed to invest every year to hit my FI goals. This was the spreadsheet that I showed Woody when I wanted to demonstrate for him that FI was possible for us. It's also the same spreadsheet I used to help validate that quitting my job after having Blake to pursue entrepreneurship full-time was possible. What would it do to our finances if we weren't able to contribute or invest for five years? How far out would that push our FI goals?

In this phase, you're simply gathering information and creating a starting point for your FI plan and you are creating an initial end point based on what you know now. By understanding your current financial situation, including your income, expenses, debts, and assets, as well as your mindset and habits, you can determine where you are now and what steps are necessary to reach your desired goals. This information will allow you to map out a personalized plan for achieving FI and your ideal lifestyle. If you are doing this with a partner, you'd combine income, joint expenses, debt, and assets in this phase.

WHAT YOU NEED TO KNOW

You'll need to know the following metrics in order to start creating your initial plan:

- Current Income

- Current Expenses

- Current Assets

- Current Liabilities

- Future Expected Income in FI

- Future Expenses in FI

- Future Assets to Cover Expenses in FI

- Future Liabilities in FI

It's impossible to determine what adjustments are necessary

without a clear understanding of your current situation and numbers. This is why it's essential to examine all the tangible aspects of the FI formula and record your financial figures. This helps you understand your true starting point and helps you figure out your end point.

The purpose of this step is to bring awareness to your financial status and provide an accurate snapshot of your financial situation. After becoming aware of your financial status, the second step is to make appropriate changes and tweaks to optimize the tangible components which you'll do in Part 3. Some changes can be made immediately, while others may take time. Cutting expenses or earning more money sustainably may take time and effort, such as taking classes or finding a higher-paying job.

Ignorance Is *Not* Bliss

While this is an exciting part of the FI planning process, it can also feel overwhelming as we really start to look at your numbers. I want to encourage you that knowing where you are is better than ignoring or avoiding your current reality. Ignorance is expensive. When it comes to your finances, not knowing important information is not bliss but costly. While it may feel easier and less painful to avoid knowing where you stand for fear of an uncomfortable truth, staying willfully ignorant will not take the pain away, but compound it until you can no longer ignore it. The cost is usually a missed opportunity to earn more or the time to have your money work for you in a way that does bring you happiness. Whether it's staying in debt longer than necessary, or delaying investing because you didn't feel like you had enough but in reality you did, you can no longer afford to not know. It's costing you not only money but also valuable time that can't be regained.

Knowing where you are with your income and expenses will be transformative. Just the act of knowing where you stand, even if you don't like where you are, brings you closer to your goal of financial freedom than not knowing. Knowledge is power and puts you in the game vs. being on the sideline, missing the game completely.

YOUR CURRENT INCOME

To understand the opportunity for growth and increasing your income, you first must know your current income. This can be pretty simple if you have a fixed income at a salaried or set hourly wage job and are paid on a consistent basis, such as every two weeks. If you're a gig worker or employed in a more creative or unpredictable per-hour work environment that doesn't provide a fixed income (that is, you have a variable income), you'll need to document your current income on a weekly or monthly basis. Just as you would have combined any joint expenses if you are combining your finances with a partner, you would look at your joint income and later on joint expenses too.

Income Sources

- W-2 from an employer

- Side hustle

- Real estate

- Investments

If you're counting income from real estate or side hustles,

include any associated expenses in your expenses tracking. For instance, if you're counting real estate rental income, include any related expenses, such as repairs, property taxes, and so forth.

Variable Income

Variable income can be assessed in two ways, similar to the options for calculating expenses: looking backward and tracking forward. If you have variable income, look back at your past income. How much can you reasonably expect to bring in as a minimum, based on your most recent income history and future expectations? For variable income, I suggest looking at the previous three months in weekly increments, since payments between weeks can fluctuate.

Alternatively, you can track your income going forward over the course of a month.

YOUR CURRENT EXPENSES

Let's look at your actual expenses because it's difficult to accurately assess them without seeing the numbers.

Understanding Your Expenses Categories

To better manage your finances, you must understand where your money is going each month. To analyze your current expenses, consider the types of expenses you have and how they impact your finances. By examining the amount, predictability, necessity, and frequency of your expenses, you can make more informed decisions about your spending and create a more realistic budget. Let's take a closer look at how to evaluate your expenses. The two main ways in which we will be looking at your expenses are:

- Expense Necessity (mandatory or discretionary): Is the expense a mandatory expense that you need to pay in order to survive and fulfill work obligations (e.g., paying for housing, food, transportation to get to work, etc.) or a discretionary expense that is not needed for survival or work?

- Expense Amount Predictability (fixed or variable): Is the expense fixed, meaning the payment amount is always the same each time, or is it variable, meaning that the payment amount fluctuates?

We will also take note of the third attribute of an expense, frequency, which will help with planning your spending moving forward. Expense frequency is how often you pay for that expense—e.g., one time per day, one or two times per month, one time per year?

Main Types of Expenses

Mandatory expenses are expenses that are necessary to your life and survival (or are obligations you must pay like minimum debt payments).

Discretionary expenses are nice to have but aren't necessary for your survival.

Fixed expenses are the same amount each month or have the same payment frequency.

Variable expenses change and/or fluctuate from month to month.

EXAMPLES OF
THE FOUR EXPENSE CATEGORIES

	FIXED	VARIABLE
MANDATORY	Mortgage or rent, renter's/auto insurance	Groceries, fuel
DISCRETIONARY	Monthly massage, gym membership	Going out to eat with friends, non-work related clothing purchases

First, let's look at your current expenses. If you've never done an exercise like this, it may seem overwhelming. On the other side of feeling overwhelmed is knowledge and power. If you've been avoiding looking at your expenses, remember that ignorance about what's happening with your finances—and in particular, your expenses—can be costly. You may be working more and spending more money than you need to. If that's the case, don't you want to find out now?

Once you know where you stand with your expenses, you'll have a clear sense of where you are on your financial journey. After reviewing everything, you may find easy and quick ways to save money. Or maybe you'll decide that you don't want to or can't cut out anything. That's fine too. But you'll be consciously making that decision instead of feeling like you have no control over your situation. If you decide you don't want to change anything about your expenses, you'll need to fully focus on increasing your income, which we'll talk about in the next chapter.

Now I'll share two different ways to track or record your expenses: the Looking Back Method and the Looking Forward Method.

Get the most updated version of these resources and other tools via your complimentary Your Journey to Financial Freedom Toolkit at www.yourjourneytofinancialfreedom.com.

MORE EXAMPLES OF EXPENSES

Mandatory Fixed:

- Childcare/Daycare
- Cell Phone
- Internet
- Minimum Debt Payments

Mandatory Variable:

- Utility Bills
- Auto Tolls, Parking, Rideshare
- Household Goods/Toiletries

Discretionary Fixed:

- Home Cleaning Service
- Home Gardening Service
- Magazine/Software Subscriptions
- Streaming Services (Netflix, Spotify, etc.)

Discretionary Variable:

- Grooming—Haircuts/Salon/Waxing and Nails

- Alcohol

- Restaurants

- Entertainment and Outings (movies, music shows, etc.)

Additional Debt Payments:

- Additional Credit Card Payment

- Additional Mortgage Payment

- Additional Student Loan Payment

- Additional Car Loan Payment

Saving and Investing Contributions:

- Savings (emergency fund, FU savings, house down payment)

- Travel

- Investing (Traditional IRA, Roth IRA, taxable account contributions)

The following expenses occur infrequently. For instance, auto repairs do not happen every month, but if you own a car, you will inevitably spend money on its maintenance. While you cannot foresee when your car will require a repair for a flat tire, you can anticipate when it will need an oil change. Later, in the "budgeting" section, I will illustrate how to allocate funds to sinking funds and rainy day categories, which will enable you to have enough money set aside to cover these expenses.

Examples of Infrequent Expenses:

- Auto—Maintenance and Repairs

- Home Maintenance

- Medical

- Pet—Vet

- Clothes

- Donations

- Furniture

- Gifts for Others

- Massage and Wellness

- Christmas and Holidays

Option 1: The Looking Backward Method

Look back at your expenses for the past three months. Looking back also helps you to calculate the average of your variable expenses. If one month was unusual because you happened to celebrate three birthdays and thus had higher expenses, but the other two months show lower expenses, then you can get a true sense of your spending. The advantage to this method is that you have the data you need to set up a plan and start making changes now. The disadvantage of this method is that it might seem like a daunting task to collect all the necessary information.

Gather: Log in to your bank and credit card accounts to see your transaction history and collect any statements from the previous three months.

Organize: Look at your expenses for the last three months and sort them by spending category. Begin with your fixed mandatory expenses, since those usually don't change month to month, like Mortgage or Rent, and then move on to add up all the amounts you spend in areas like Groceries, Fuel, etc., that month.

Evaluate: Now that you have a full picture of your expenses by category, you can begin to determine whether you want to keep, reduce, or eliminate each expense. (You'll learn more about this in Part 3, Chapter 9 of the book.)

Option 2: The Tracking Forward Method

Another approach to gaining an understanding of your expenses is by monitoring your spending for a period of one month. This entails diligently recording and documenting all your expenses as they occur. Begin tracking your expenses starting from this point and continue for the next month. During the process of tracking your expenses, it is not necessary to make any alterations—just observe and record. If you happen to be reading this book at the beginning of the month you have an advantage! It's a great time to get started and allows you to ease your way in. A disadvantage to this method is that in order to see your complete financial picture, you'll need to wait before you implement any changes. You also may miss anomalies during the one-month tracking period, which won't give you a true sense of your spending.

Gather: Log in to your banking and credit card accounts on a consistent basis (daily or weekly), so you can record your spending activity as you go.

Organize: As you begin spending, document your expenses

and sort them by category. You can use my organizer here or paper.

Evaluate: After you've collected a month's worth of data, you can get a clear sense of how you're spending and you can begin to determine whether you want to keep, reduce, or eliminate each expense. (You'll learn more about this in Part 3 of the book.)

Your preferred method for gathering your expenses may depend on your personality. I'm the kind of person who likes to jump in feet first and can be, dare I say, a little impatient about things. Don't say you have a surprise for me and that I have to wait, because I need to know what it is right away. For me, the Look Backward Method would be my preference because I could get started right away. On the other hand, I have a friend who possesses the opposite traits in terms of patience and approach. She prefers to take her time before diving into things and is willing to wait for surprises. Her preference would be to gradually complete this and ease into it over time.

Whichever option you pick, stay committed but also recognize that it's okay to start again or try the other method if you get stuck.

Now that you have a clear picture of your current income and expenses, how do things measure up? Is your income able to cover all your expenses? Even if you're able to cover your current expenses, if you want to reach FI sooner, you'll need to find more gap, the difference between your income and expenses, so that you can put it toward your financial goals. And if that's the case, you'll need to increase your income or decrease your expenses or do a combination of both.

BUDGETING

A budget allows you to see and manage your cash flow. It also helps you track what money comes in (income) and what money goes out (expenses). If you don't already have a budget, you will create one as we progress through the next sections.

Now that you know your current expenses and income you can create a budget that will help you stay accountable to reaching your financial and life goals. A budget is a plan that tells your money where to go. Creating and sticking to a budget is an essential part of the beginning stages of your financial journey. That said, you can decide the type of budgeting system you use, whether it's on a spreadsheet, an app, or just pen and paper. As you go through this process, you may eventually find that you don't need to use a budget in the same way or with the same intensity. When I first started to get serious about my finances and started to document my journey publicly, I was all about budgeting. Before I changed the name of my blog to *Journey to Launch* it was called *Mrs-BudgetFab* if that shows you how committed I was to a budget. At work, I'd have my budget pulled up in a tab, updating the numbers as much as I could so it could be accurate. It was actually fun for me at the time because I knew that managing my money in this intense way would lead me out of my dark cubicle era (I didn't sit near a window at the time so the area was literally dark) into the sunshine. I was uncomfortable enough with my life situation that finding a way to make it better through my finances made me appreciate and lean into budgeting.

Budgeting for some, including my younger self, was a means to an end. Now that I'm in the Commander stage and in a comfortable place, I no longer use budgeting in the same way. I'm confident in my ability to spend without sabotaging my long-term goals and for now, I've let go of my obsession with my budget and accounting for every dollar. I prioritize my investing goals first by automatically transferring money into my investment accounts and spend the rest on mandatory and discretionary expenses. As long as we are hitting our investing goals and we can comfortably pay our bills and credit cards in full every month it works for us, for now. However, if our situation or goals were to change and we needed to go back to a stricter budgeting style, we would.

If you are feeling overwhelmed with the idea of having to stick to a budget for the rest of your life which then prevents you from starting one, I'm here to tell you that you don't have to commit to a strict budgeting style for your entire journey. I didn't.

You may on the other hand find that you need to have a strict budget in place in order for you to not only make the progress you want to see but to also maintain it. I know some people who LOVE to budget because of the sense of control and security of knowing where every dollar is going. But if you are at the beginning Journeyer stages, for example, an Explorer looking to get some stability, or a Cadet looking to become consumer debt-free, a budget will serve as a fuel booster, accelerating the time it takes to reach these goals because you can become more intentional with your money, expanding the gap between your income and expenses to make significant progress.

I remember first joining my local gym; I only took the group classes because I needed the energy and accountability from others to do my best workout. I felt more inclined to work harder when I was surrounded by others and with an instructor telling me what to do. I never imagined doing workouts on my own or lifting weights outside of the classes. Over time, the classes became a little less convenient, which made me realize how much time I could save by working out according to my own schedule. I also discovered that I could enhance the effectiveness of my workouts by focusing on specific exercises that aligned with my personal goals, rather than following someone else's instructions. As a result, I currently find myself in a phase of my life where I am pursuing my own workout routines, for now. I feel so empowered knowing that I can choose what method is best for me depending on the day, group workouts or solo workouts. That's how I want you to feel with budgeting or any other skillset you learn as you move forward on your journey. You should feel empowered to try new things, feel confident enough to take action and make mistakes, and feel equipped with the necessary tools to get the result you want.

Ariana, who was on episode 294 of the podcast, is a long-time Journeyer and was also a part of my membership community. Ariana struggled to find a budgeting system that worked. She tried budgeting with paper and pen, Excel, and even the budget apps, but found it confusing. "I've tried so many different apps, and they all wind up just annoying me. And after two or three months, I'm just like, I'm done with all of this. I've also recently been diagnosed with ADHD and like, the act of going through my expenses, and like earmarking things, drives me absolutely insane. And now it makes sense why budgeting in that way was so hard for me." Ariana is now working with a percent budget that automatically uses percentages to put toward her major budgeting categories. Ariana has a percentage of her income go into her checking account to be spent on discretionary spending, and then her checking account guides her decision-making. If she doesn't have enough in the account or knows she has upcoming expenses she will help use that as guidance for how she spends. The bills, her savings, and paying off debt are automated, which allows her to simplify her budget.

Whether you use a zero-based budget or a percentage-based budget, or use an old-fashioned pen and paper to write out your budget or budget app, find the system and budgeting style that best serves you. The important thing is that you establish a cash-flow system that helps you feel confident and in control of where your money is going and allows you to reach your goals.

ZERO-BASED BUDGETING

For the purpose of this book, I'll be going over the zero-based budget method. The zero-based budget directs every dollar that comes in to a specific job. With this budgeting method, you assign every dollar of your income a specific purpose and allocate your income to the various categories or expenses so that your income minus expenses equals zero. Think about it as if you are the general of your army, and the dollars that come in are your soldiers. In order to complete your intended mission, you have to tell them what to do in advance because otherwise there will be chaos. The soldiers will end up telling you what to do and you will have no control.

Let's go over the steps to start a zero-based budget.

1. Before the next month starts or at the top of the month, write out or use an app to start your new month's budget. Every month is an opportunity for a fresh start, but you will have to deal with or close out any carryover activity from the previous month.

2. Write out how much you are assigning to each budget category for the month.

3. Set up time in advance when you are going to review your budget and update your spending activity to what you assigned so that it's up-to-date and put it in your calendar. Make sure to make these budgeting sessions comfortable for yourself. Grab your favorite beverage, put on some music if you like. Make it an enjoyable experience. If you are doing this with a partner, make sure to find a time that works for both of you. You can choose once a week or twice a month. If you're new to budgeting, do it frequently until you establish a routine and reach your desired level of proficiency. Waiting until the end of the month to update your budget can be overwhelming and insufficient in providing you with the necessary information to make informed decisions throughout the month. The purpose of a budget is not only to reflect on past spending but also to enable better decision-making and adjustment for future expenses. This is why checking your budget regularly is crucial. Dealing with six to ten transactions a week will be more manageable than dealing with forty transactions at month's end. Additionally,

if you use cash for purchases, budgeting frequently can help avoid confusion over what the cash was spent on or the purpose of a particular charge.

4. Reconcile your budget and keep up-to-date with your spending. Reconciling your budget involves comparing your budgeted amounts for each spending category with the actual amount you spent in that category during a given period of time (such as a week or a month). By reconciling your budget, you can identify areas where you may have overspent or underspent, and make adjustments for the future.

5. Utilize the information from your budget to help you in making informed spending choices. For instance, if you exceed your budgeted amount in one category, consider which line item you can draw from to offset that overspending. Alternatively, if you have unspent funds in a particular category, consider redirecting those funds toward other areas where you may need them more.

For your savings or blow money—funds you can spend at your own discretion on anything you want—you can roll that money forward from month to month. For example, if you assign $200 in your January blow money category and only use $140 of it in January, then you can allocate the unused $60 to your February blow budget line item which gives you a total of $260 to spend however you want in February.

Digital budgets work well for keeping track of unused funds and for categorizing your spending for you because they can connect directly with your bank account and automatically import your transactions.

Blow Money or **Fun Money** is a line item I add in my budget to account for spending on things I want for the fun of it and without justification. If you have a last-minute meetup with friends that isn't covered by your restaurant line item, or you decide to make a random purchase at Target, you can assign the money to that category.

Rainy-Day or **Sinking Fund** are expenses that occur irregularly, such as furniture purchases, car maintenance, and birthday gifts. Since you anticipate these expenses throughout the year or once a year, it's beneficial to save for them over a period of time. To determine the monthly savings amount, divide the estimated annual expense by twelve or by the number of months until the payment is due. For example, if you plan to spend $1,200 on Christmas gifts for your entire family, you'd set aside $100 each month, starting in January. Similarly, if your average yearly car maintenance cost is $800, you'd allocate $67 per month. This approach also can save you money when you want to make upfront payments for certain items, such as car insurance, to obtain a discount.

The Assigned column is how much money you are putting towards that budget line item for the month. The Activity column is how much you have used of that money for the month. The Available column is how much is left over to be used for that budget category. For example, some things like Rent/Mortgage you'll pay for one time at the start of the month so there will be nothing left over in the Available category. For things like groceries, you may assign $500 to that category and by the 15th of the month spent $250, so your activity would show $250 and there will be $250 in the Available column left for you to spend that month.

For expenses that you pay annually or every six months like car insurance or renter's insurance, you can either note the month that the annual payment is due so you are aware that you need to pay for it or you can break the expected future payment up into twelve payments and save for it in advance over time, just like the sinking fund category. If you know that you have to pay $1200 in car insurance for the year in January of the next year and it is now January, you can begin to put $100 in the Assigned category every month and as each month passes, your Available amount will grow until it hits $1,200 a month, now you know that you have $1,200 earmarked to pay for your car insurance when the time comes. You can keep that money in a separate savings account or your checking account depending on your preference but your budget and the Available column tells you what your money is already earmarked for in your accounts.

EXAMPLE BUDGET TEMPLATE

Budget Month: _____	Income: _____		
Recurring Expense	Assigned	Activity	Available
Rent/Mortgage	$0.00	$0.00	$0.00
Childcare Expenses	$0.00	$0.00	$0.00
Renter's Insurance	$0.00	$0.00	$0.00

Budget Month: _____	Income: _____		
Recurring Expense	Assigned	Activity	Available
Utility—Garbage	$0.00	$0.00	$0.00
Utility—Gas and Electric	$0.00	$0.00	$0.00
Utility—Water	$0.00	$0.00	$0.00
Auto—Insurance	$0.00	$0.00	$0.00
Auto—Gas	$0.00	$0.00	$0.00
Auto—Tolls, Parking, Rideshare	$0.00	$0.00	$0.00
Groceries	$0.00	$0.00	$0.00
Household Goods/Toiletries	$0.00	$0.00	$0.00
Cell Phone	$0.00	$0.00	$0.00
Internet	$0.00	$0.00	$0.00
Grooming—Haircuts/Salon/ Waxing and Nails	$0.00	$0.00	$0.00
Home Cleaning Service	$0.00	$0.00	$0.00
Home Gardening Service	$0.00	$0.00	$0.00
Alcohol and Bars	$0.00	$0.00	$0.00
Restaurants	$0.00	$0.00	$0.00
Entertainment (Movies, Music Shows, etc.)	$0.00	$0.00	$0.00
Magazine/Software Subscriptions	$0.00	$0.00	$0.00
Fitness	$0.00	$0.00	$0.00
Streaming Services (Netflix, Spotify, etc.)	$0.00	$0.00	$0.00
Other	$0.00	$0.00	$0.00
Total	$0.00	$0.00	$0.00
Rainy Day/Sinking Funds			
Auto—Maintenance and Repairs	$0.00	$0.00	$0.00
Home Maintenance	$0.00	$0.00	$0.00
Medical	$0.00	$0.00	$0.00

Budget Month: _____	Income: _____		
Recurring Expense	Assigned	Activity	Available
Pet—Vet	$0.00	$0.00	$0.00
Clothes	$0.00	$0.00	$0.00
Donations	$0.00	$0.00	$0.00
Furniture	$0.00	$0.00	$0.00
Gifts for Others	$0.00	$0.00	$0.00
Massage and Wellness	$0.00	$0.00	$0.00
Christmas and Holidays	$0.00	$0.00	$0.00
Other	$0.00	$0.00	$0.00
Total	$0.00	$0.00	$0.00
Debt Payments			
Student Loan	$0.00	$0.00	$0.00
Credit Card	$0.00	$0.00	$0.00
Car Loan	$0.00	$0.00	$0.00
Other	$0.00	$0.00	$0.00
Total	$0.00	$0.00	$0.00
Saving and Investing Goals			
Savings (Emergency Fund, FU Savings)	$0.00	$0.00	$0.00
Travel	$0.00	$0.00	$0.00
Taxable Investing	$0.00	$0.00	$0.00
Other	$0.00	$0.00	$0.00
Total	$0.00	$0.00	$0.00
Grand Total	$0.00	$0.00	$0.00

YOUR CURRENT ASSETS

Assets are things that you own. They have value and can provide you with security for today and income that will one day cover your expenses in the future.

Assets include:

- Balances in tax-advantaged retirement investments accounts like 401(k)s, 403(b)s, 457s, Traditional IRAs, Roth IRAs (these accounts provide a tax benefit and you may have to pay a penalty if you withdraw before standard retirement age).

- Balances in non-retirement taxable investments accounts (these accounts have no tax advantage and can be used whenever you want without penalty, you'd just pay taxes on withdrawals).

- Balances in bank accounts

- Cash

- Value of real estate including both primary home and investment properties

- Other types of investment accounts (REITs, HSAs, cash value of permanent life insurance policies)

YOUR CURRENT LIABILITIES

Liabilities or debt are things you owe, including:

- Credit card debt

- Car loans

- Mortgages—primary home, investment properties

- Personal loans

- Student loans

Create a complete list of your debts to see how much you owe. Write out the following for each consumer debt you have:

- Name of creditor

- Minimum monthly payment

- Outstanding debt

- Interest rate

You can include your mortgage just to have all of your debt information in one place and to help you figure out your net worth but for the purposes of paying off your debt we will focus on your non-mortgage debt. You can choose to pay off your mortgage early AFTER you've paid off all of your consumer debt and are caught up in retirement savings.

Now you should know the following to get a clear sense of your starting point:

- Your Current Income

- Your Current Expenses

- Your Current Assets

- Your Current Liabilities

CALCULATING YOUR FI NUMBER: THE 25X RULE AND 4% RULE

In order to create the plan to reach financial independence, you'll need to calculate how much to save and how much you'll be able to take from your portfolio on an annual basis to fulfill your financially independent lifestyle. We will be briefly going over two rules of thumb that will help us quickly figure out how to calculate these numbers—the 25x Rule and the 4% Withdrawal Rule. We can work to figure out (1) the total amount you need to have based on the lifestyle and expenses you want to spend—using the 25x multiplier rule and (2) How much income your current investments can provide for you using the 4% Withdrawal Rule. Both rules of thumb use a thirty-year time horizon. There are other more sophisticated and accurate ways to figure how much you'll truly need, but for now, it's just important to get a sense of how much you need without the complicated jargon or math. At this stage of the journey it's important to remove barriers that prevent you from starting such as having to understand every single component or investment term or finding the perfect formula to calculate an end number that probably will change anyway.

25x Rule

To get a general sense of what your target financial independence number will be, take the desired amount you want to spend annually in your FI years and multiply it by 25. You can use your current annual expense and adjust it accordingly for what you think you may need when you reach FI. For example, consider if your mortgage will be paid off by then, which would eliminate that expense, or if you need to allocate more money for health care and travel expenses.

4% Withdrawal Rule

To figure out how much you can spend on an annual basis based on how much you have in your investment portfolio, we will use something called the 4% Withdrawal Rule. Simply multiply your total investment portfolio by 4% and it will give you the annual amount you can withdraw from your portfolio for the next thirty years without running out of money. How is it that you don't run out of money? The investment returns that your portfolio incurs will outlast the withdrawals you make for at least thirty years because of compound interest and investment returns.

The 4% Rule is attributed to Bill Bengen, a financial adviser in Southern California who created it in the mid-1990s. He created it using historical data on stock and bond returns over the fifty-year period from 1926 to 1976, focusing on the severe market downturns of the 1930s and early 1970s. Bengen concluded that, even during unsustainable markets, no historical case existed in which a 4% annual withdrawal exhausted a retirement portfolio in less than thirty-three years.

| ANNUAL EXPENSES | x (times) | 25 | = (equals) | FI NUMBER—AMOUNT NEEDED IN RETIREMENT & INVESTMENT ACCOUNTS |

$$\$40,000 \times 25 = \$1,000,000$$
$$\$75,000 \times 25 = \$1,875,000$$
$$\$100,000 \times 25 = \$2,500,000$$

With the 25x Rule, the more money you need and want to

spend means the more you'll need to have saved and invested in your investment accounts.

Now let's look at the 4% withdrawal rate in action. Let's say you have some money already invested and want to see how much of an annual income that money can provide you.

 x (times) **=** (equals) **ANNUAL AMOUNT YOU CAN DRAW DOWN FROM YOUR RETIREMENT AND INVESTMENT ACCOUNTS**

$100,000 x 4% = $4,000
$250,000 x 4% = $10,000

$500,000 x 4% = $20,000
$750,000 x 4% = $30,000

$1,000,000 x 4% = $40,000
$1,875,000 x 4% = $75,000

Critics who push back against the rules claim that they are either too conservative or not conservative enough. One even more conservative school of thought suggests that multiplying your expenses by 25 is not sufficient and suggests that you should multiply your annual expense number by 30. This approach requires you to have more money in case of volatile market returns, inflation, and unforeseen life events in the future like health care needs that will require you to spend more money.

The same conservative approach can be applied to the withdrawal rate. Instead of using the 4% withdrawal, you aim for 3%, which will make you draw down less of your portfolio over time. Even Bill Bengen, the originator of the 4% Rule, has since said that a more realistic withdrawal rate would be 5% of your portfolio.

What you deem as too aggressive or too conservative is going to be based on your individual circumstances and perspective. Your desired Guac level and risk tolerance will determine what your FI number and expected withdrawal rate will be. Here's the other thing, whatever multiple or percent you decide to use now will change again in the future. You will also most likely change your mind about how aggressive or conservative you want to be as you move forward because with experience and time comes more information and knowing of what you truly want out of your life.

You should also be looking at your financial independence number and take into account future sources of income that can reduce the amount you'd need to have saved and invested for your early retirement goals or standard retirement goals. For example, if you expect to receive a pension through your job or expect your rental properties to be debt-free in retirement where you can collect and apply the rent as part of your income, you can factor that into your calculation of how much you'd need.

If you expect to receive a $40,000 pension in the future and you've calculated that you want to spend $80,000 in your FI years your FI number would be 2,000,000 (80,000 x 25 = 2,000,000). You would only need to have half of that by the time you can access that pension (let's say fifty-nine). So, by the time you're fifty-nine, you'd need at least $1,000,000 in invested assets in addition to your pension to help support your $80,000 a year expense lifestyle. You can figure out how much you need to invest to accumulate $1,000,000 by the age of fifty-nine, which would be significantly less than what you'd need to invest to get to a portfolio of $2,000,000. Which means you can spend more money on things that you care about now. However, since your pension would be tied to actually working at the job you may not be able to quit early without losing all or some of it.

When you begin to think about your expenses in the future, you'll also have to consider how your budget will change; maybe your mortgage will be paid off and your kids will be older so that would eliminate some of your highest expenses, but then you factor in more money for health care and travel. Use your current budget as a starting point and add in line items or take out things you think you may not need. Creating this future budget allows you to see how much income you'll need to bring in from your investments—which in turn tells you the FI number you'll need to aim for—or other sources to sustain your lifestyle.

While we are focusing a lot on the numbers right now, financial independence encompasses more than a mere figure or the amount of funds in your account. There are people who reach their financial independence number and still don't feel financially secure. Your perspective and mindset toward your finances play a significant role in your feeling of financial security, which is why it's crucial to explore ways to feel secure and attain freedom prior to reaching complete financial independence. Imagine feeling secure even though you have debt or while being what seems to be far off from reaching your FI number because you have confidence in your ability to learn and do what you need to do in order to move yourself closer to your goal. So many of the variables will change over time as you pursue this goal and that is the point of this journey because as you continue forward you will uncover what things matter the most to you and how you want to live your life.

These calculations and rules of thumb are simply meant to give you your initial targets because if we are going to do this and journey forward, we have to at least know the direction and have an initial target that we are aiming toward. Your real number and the lifestyle you want will change over time as you gather more information. The number doesn't have to be precise, instead use it as your initial target so that it allows you to have some direction in where you are going.

If you take what you want your future expenses to be to reach financial independence, what number do you come up with? You can use your current expenses that you figured out as a baseline to get a rough number. Before you throw this book down at the thought of doing this calculation and how much the number is—take a deep breath. This exercise, for most people, will scare the hell out of them, like it did me.

HOW LONG YOU WANT IT TO TAKE VS. HOW LONG IT ACTUALLY TAKES

When I first found out about the FIRE movement and did the quick 25x Rule calculation based on what I thought we wanted to spend in retirement, I was in shock. I thought spending $100,000 a year would suffice to cover our needs, but that meant we'd require a $2,500,000 portfolio ($100,000 x 25). If I planned on working until I was sixty, that would have definitely been possible, but I wanted to reach financial independence in seven years, by the time I was forty years old. At the time, we had nowhere close to that amount invested, and there would be no way that we could reach that $2,500,000 target portfolio in seven years. It felt impossible based on our current numbers and the aggressive time frame. After my disbelief somewhat wore off, I regretted not taking investing more seriously earlier in my working career. I distinctly remember clicking through my 401(k) employee account when I started working full-time and selecting 0% contribution because I wanted all of my money NOW, not caring about what old and gray-haired Jamila would need, that was her problem and she'd figured it out then. That twenty-two-year-old Jamila had a life to live and needed all of her money. Thirty-three-year-old Jamila was seeing the results of my twenty-two-year-old self's decisions.

Once the shock and disbelief wore off, I realized that I was asking and answering the wrong type of questions. I didn't know enough to ask myself if reaching financial independence was possible in seven years. It wasn't "Can I reach this goal?" I should have been asking myself the better question: "How can I reach this goal? And If I fail at attempting this goal, will I be better or worse off than where I am today?" Later on I had an even better question that would demand a more thoughtful and creative approach to how I would go about solving for the answer: "Why is it important to reach this goal?" Changing the questions I asked myself and changing the questions you ask yourself around the goals you will set for yourself matter. The question of "Can I reach this?" only gave me black-and-white answers of yes or no, and at my starting point, I didn't know enough to be able to confidently answer that question in a positive way. But the other questions that started with "How," "Why," and "If" made me think more creatively and gave me hope.

You'll need that same hope and faith as you calculate your number.

The speed that you'll be able to reach your FI number will depend on the six components we talked about earlier (income, expenses, liabilities, assets, mindset, habits) and using your income to do its four jobs (pay for mandatory expenses, reduce liabilities, increase assets, pay for discretionary expenses) correctly and efficiently.

You can try out different FI budgets by visualizing what your life could look like at different Guac levels. Come up with a range of FI numbers based on a basic lifestyle. How much would you need if your budget was more bare-bones and mostly mandatory expenses (Guac level 1 or 2) and what would you need if you wanted to spend more (Guac 3 and up?). Coming up with a range of FI numbers is helpful because then it allows you to envision what your FI life could look like at the various levels and see if you want to have to save or invest more to get there.

GUAC LEVEL LIFESTYLES AND YOUR FI NUMBER

ANNUAL EXPENSES	x (times)	25	= (equals)	FI NUMBER—AMOUNT NEEDED IN RETIREMENT & INVESTMENT ACCOUNTS

GUAC 1 OR 2:
$40,000 x 25 = $1,000,000

GUAC 3:
$75,000 x 25 = $1,875,000

GUAC 4 OR 5:
$100,000 x 25 = $2,500,000

FI PLAN EXAMPLE: MARCY

Now that we've gathered all the components and numbers necessary to craft your FI plan, let's look at how this all works together using Marcy as an example. Like you, Marcy wants to reach FI sooner rather than later and has completed an assessment of her current finances. She knows the following:

Marcy's Starting Point

- Current Income: $4,000

- Current Expenses: $3,800 (includes minimum debt payments and any savings goals)

- Current Gap: $200 the difference between income and expenses, but because she hasn't been budgeting that money quickly disappears to random expenses or sits in her checking account

- Current Liabilities: $9,000 in credit card debt

- Current Assets: $250 in savings account and $6,000 in 401(k) account

Marcy's Desired End Goal

- Future Expenses: $4,500 a month

- FI Number or Future Assets to Cover Expenses in FI: 648,000

- FI number based on the 25x Rule is = $4.500 * 12= $54,000 and $54,000 * 12 = 648,000

- Marcy is currently 28 years old and wants to reach FI/ early retirement in 10 years.

Can she do it? Let's see:

Marcy has the basic information she needs to start crafting a plan and to play around with different scenarios to see what's possible for her. In her plan, she'll need to incorporate paying off her $9,000 debt and saving in her emergency fund.

We are now going to compare four different scenarios where we can see what Marcy's FI plan looks like if she (1) takes no action, her current way, (2) makes changes to create an $800 gap, (3) creates an even bigger gap of $2,000, and (4) a scenario where she can't invest consistently and has to delay the start of her FI plan. For all scenarios, a 6% return rate is assumed.

Scenario 1: No Changes

Assuming Marcy makes no changes to her financial situation and maintains her current course, she will have $51,000 by the age of sixty-five. This projection takes into account the fact that she does not contribute any additional funds to her 401(k), which currently holds $6,000. This amount will grow to slightly over $51,000 by the time Marcy reaches sixty-four years of age, thanks to the effects of compound interest.

Age	Total Forecasted	Pre-Tax Retirement Contributions
28	$6,000	$0
29	$6,360	$0
30	$6,743	$0
31	$7,148	$0
32	$7,577	$0
33	$8,032	$0
34	$8,514	$0
35	$9,025	$0
36	$9,567	$0
37	$10,141	$0
38	$10,750	$0
39	$11,395	$0
40	$12,079	$0
41	$12,804	$0
42	$13,572	$0
43	$14,387	$0
44	$15,250	$0
45	$16,165	$0
46	$17,135	$0
47	$18,163	$0
48	$19,252	$0
49	$20,407	$0
50	$21,632	$0
51	$22,930	$0
52	$24,305	$0
53	$25,763	$0
54	$27,309	$0
55	$28,947	$0
56	$30,684	$0
57	$32,524	$0
58	$34,475	$0
59	$36,543	$0
60	$38,736	$0
61	$41,059	$0
62	$43,522	$0
63	$46,133	$0
64	$48,901	$0
65	$51,834	$0

Scenario 2: Baseline Changes

Now let's say Marcy begins to use some of the methods in this book like increasing her income, optimizing her expenses and budgeting to help give her a $800 gap. She uses the percent guide on how to use the money in the gap by Journeyer stage in Chapter 4.

HOW TO DISBURSE THE GAP
To Reach Financial & Lifestyle Goals

JOURNEYER LEVEL	Explorer	Cadet	Aviator	Commander	Captain
Debt Payoff		50%			
Savings		20%	30%		
Investing		20%	50%	50%	
Discretionary Expenses		10%	20%	50%	100%
SUM:		100%	100%	100%	100%

NOTE: The Explorer category is empty because the main priority of the Explorer is to pay for your mandatory expenses.

Using the percent as a guideline of how to break up money in the $800 gap between saving, investing, and paying off debt that I showed you earlier, Marcy figures out that while she is in the Cadet stage, she can put $160 toward saving, $400 toward additional debt payments, $160 toward investing, and $80 to put toward discretionary expenses. Once she pays off her consumer debt and moves from the Cadet stage to the Aviator stage, she can redistribute the $400 that she was using to pay off debt to investing and discretionary expenses.

EXAMPLE #1 OF HOW YOU
WOULD DISTRIBUTE $800 GAP
According to Journeyer Level

JOURNEYER LEVEL	Explorer	Cadet	Aviator	Commander	Captain
$800					
Debt Payoff		$400	$0	$0	$0
Savings		$160	$240	$0	$0
Investing		$160	$400	$400	$0
Discretionary Expenses		$80	$160	$400	$800
SUM:		$800	$800	$800	$800

NOTE: The Explorer category is empty because the main priority of the Explorer is to pay for your mandatory expenses.

Assuming Marcy doesn't get into any more debt, it would take her about three years to pay off her credit card debt and then six years to save up to her fully funded emergency fund. As you can see in the chart, she only invests $160 a month, or $1,920 a year for the first three years and then is able to invest the $400 a month or $4,800 a year moving forward and is able to accumulate $651,000 by sixty-five years old.

Let's map out what her FI plan looks like now:

Age	Total Forecasted	Pre-Tax Retirement Contributions
28	$6,000	$1,920
29	$8,396	$1,920
30	$10,935	$1,920
31	$16,680	$4,800
32	$22,769	$4,800
33	$29,223	$4,800
34	$36,065	$4,800
35	$43,317	$4,800
36	$51,005	$4,800
37	$59,153	$4,800
38	$67,790	$4,800
39	$76,946	$4,800
40	$86,651	$4,800
41	$96,938	$4,800
42	$107,843	$4,800
43	$119,401	$4,800
44	$131,653	$4,800
45	$144,641	$4,800
46	$158,407	$4,800
47	$172,999	$4,800
48	$188,467	$4,800
49	$204,863	$4,800
50	$222,243	$4,800
51	$240,665	$4,800
52	$260,193	$4,800
53	$280,892	$4,800
54	$302,834	$4,800
55	$326,091	$4,800
56	$350,745	$4,800
57	$376,877	$4,800
58	$404,577	$4,800
59	$433,939	$4,800
60	$465,063	$4,800
61	$498,055	$4,800
62	$533,026	$4,800
63	$570,095	$4,800
64	$609,388	$4,800
65	$651,038	$4,800

Scenario 3: Bigger Gap

If Marcy begins implementing and working on all the things we talked about in this book, especially working on increasing her income, she can easily turn the $800 gap into $2,000 over time. Let's see how a $2,000 gap would be distributed according to the percent guidelines.

EXAMPLE #2 OF HOW YOU WOULD DISTRIBUTE $2,000 GAP
According to Journeyer Level

JOURNEYER LEVEL	Explorer	Cadet	Aviator	Commander	Captain
$2,000					
Debt Payoff		$1,000	$0	$0	$0
Savings		$400	$600	$0	$0
Investing		$400	$1,000	$1,000	$0
Discretionary Expenses		$200	$400	$1,000	$2,000
SUM:		$2,000	$2,000	$2,000	$2,000

NOTE: The Explorer category is empty because the main priority of the Explorer is to pay for your mandatory expenses.

Let's assume that it takes her three years to work on the components and increase her gap to $2,000, and she is not able to invest a full $1,000 a month until she is thirty-one years old. For the sake of simplicity, let's also assume that it takes her three years to pay off her debt and six years to build up her emergency fund, even though in reality these timelines would likely be significantly shorter once she increases her gap. If she could grow her gap to $2,000 where she could invest $1,000 a month or $12,000 a year, she can reach her FI number by fifty-three years old, accumulating $639,564 in her investment accounts, shaving twelve years off her FI journey compared to the previous scenario of the $800 gap. If she actually found work she loved and didn't want to stop working (that's the goal) she could keep her active income and continue to invest and have $1,501,509 by sixty-five years old.

Age	Total Forecasted	Pre-Tax Retirement Contributions
28	$6,000	$1,920
29	$8,396	$1,920
30	$10,935	$1,920
31	$24,312	$12,000
32	$38,491	$12,000
33	$53,520	$12,000
34	$69,452	$12,000
35	$86,339	$12,000
36	$104,240	$12,000
37	$123,215	$12,000
38	$143,328	$12,000
39	$164,548	$12,000
40	$187,247	$12,000
41	$211,202	$12,000
42	$236,510	$12,000
43	$263,510	$12,000
44	$292,040	$12,000
45	$322,283	$12,000
46	$354,340	$12,000
47	$388,320	$12,000
48	$424,339	$12,000
49	$462,519	$12,000
50	$502,990	$12,000
51	$545,890	$12,000
52	$591,363	$12,000
53	$639,564	$12,000
54	$690,658	$12,000
55	$744,817	$12,000
56	$802,226	$12,000
57	$863,079	$12,000
58	$927,584	$12,000
59	$995,958	$12,000
60	$1,068,435	$12,000
61	$1,226,696	$12,000
62	$1,145,261	$12,000
63	$1,226,696	$12,000
64	$1,404,518	$12,000
65	$1,501,509	$12,000

Scenario 4: Delayed Investing

Let's consider another scenario for Marcy, which we can refer to as the "delayed investing" or "ish happens" scenario, as we all know that life can throw us unexpected curveballs. What if Marcy is unable to make the financial progress she wants due to unforeseen events, or what if she is unable to find an $800 gap right away? Let's model out what that journey might look like.

Assuming it takes Marcy two years (Years 1–2) before she can start investing, and in Years 3–5 she is only able to invest $40 a month or $480 a year. Then, let's say another life event or career change occurs that impacts her finances, causing her to pause on investing for two years (Years 6–7) and not contribute anything. However, despite not being able to invest in the stock market or investment accounts during this time, Marcy can still work toward her FI goals in other ways, such as through strategic career moves and intentional money management.

Eventually, with the work she's been doing, she sees a pickup in income and is able to invest $160 a month or $1,920 a year in years 8–9. As time goes on, she continues to grow her gap and is able to invest $200 a month or $2,400 a year in Year 10 and beyond. Even with this modified and slower investing timeline, Marcy would still have $270,370 by sixty-five years old, which is still a significant improvement compared to the $51,000 she would have if she had not invested anything over that same time period. Thus, even in Marcy's worst-case scenario, she is still better off than her current situation.

Age	Total Forecasted	Pre-Tax Retirement Contributions
28	$6,000	$0
29	$6,360	$0
30	$7,251	$480
31	$8,196	$480
32	$9,197	$480
33	$9,749	$480
34	$10,334	$0
35	$12,990	$0
36	$15,804	$1,920
37	$18,788	$1,920
38	$22,460	$1,920
39	$26,351	$2,400
40	$30,477	$2,400
41	$34,849	$2,400
42	$39,484	$2,400
43	$44,398	$2,400
44	$49,606	$2,400
45	$55,126	$2,400
46	$60,977	$2,400
47	$67,180	$2,400
48	$73,755	$2,400
49	$80,724	$2,400
50	$88,111	$2,400
51	$95,942	$2,400
52	$104,242	$2,400
53	$113,040	$2,400
54	$122,367	$2,400
55	$132,252	$2,400
56	$142,731	$2,400
57	$153,839	$2,400
58	$165,613	$2,400
59	$178,093	$2,400
60	$191,322	$2,400
61	$205,345	$2,400
62	$220,209	$2,400
63	$235,965	$2,400
64	$252,667	$2,400
65	$270,370	$2,400

	SCENARIO 1: No Changes	SCENARIO 2: Changes $800 Gap	SCENARIO 3: Bigger Changes, $2,000 Gap	SCENARIO 4: Delayed Investing and Ish Happens
How Much by Sixty-five Years Old	$51,834	$651,038	$1,501,509	$270,370
FI Goal Reached?	N/A	Reaches it at sixty-five years old	Reaches it at fifty-three years old	Doesn't reach FI # but has more than she would have had by not doing anything

To reach her FI goal in the ten-year timeline she initially hoped for, Marcy would need to invest $45,000 a year from Year 1. However, this is an unrealistic goal given her current financial situation. It's not uncommon for people to set lofty FI goals for themselves, but it's important to distinguish between unrealistic expectations and big dreams. Marcy's initial goal to achieve FI in ten years was ambitious, but now that she has a better understanding of what it takes to reach that goal, she can create a practical plan that aligns with her capabilities and aspirations. She can choose to live more frugally, adjust her FI number down or work to double her income so she can invest more to reach her original target FI number. By exploring different scenarios, Marcy may decide to give herself a twenty-year timeline instead and aim to achieve FI by age forty-eight instead. She can decide now what she's willing to do to reach her goals while living her desired lifestyle and has more control over her life.

As you embark on this journey, you may be surprised at

how quickly things can change for the better. By taking action, you can gain more opportunities and clarity, and what you initially thought was impossible or would take you thirty years may only take fifteen. Alternatively, you may realize that you need to adjust your end goal and methods to achieve a more balanced life that you can enjoy now and in retirement. Any progress, even if it's not the exact outcome you envisioned in the timeline you wanted, is better than doing nothing at all. Even with a slower and more realistic investment strategy and FI timeline, Marcy has managed to invest a significant amount and build a quarter-of-a-million-dollar portfolio, which is a remarkable achievement that she should be proud of.

QUESTIONS TO ASK YOURSELF AS YOU CREATE YOUR INITIAL PLAN

As you start outlining your personalized plan, it's essential to consider the following questions. Remember, you might not have definitive answers to these questions at the moment, but it's vital to keep them in mind and revisit them as you refine your strategy along the way.

- Will you be able to depend on other income sources in retirement that will allow you to reduce your FI total number (e.g., pension, income from real estate)?

- If you have a partner, are you combining your resources, investments, income, and expenses?

- Are there any major life events coming up or that you want to prepare for that you want included in the plan?

You may want to quit a job, take a vacation, or save up for a big purchase that you need to take into account because it slows down how much you can invest or aggressively pay down debt.

- What are your lifestyle goals and can they be incorporated into your current budget? Is there something you want to add into your budget?

- Based on what you know now, are you okay with the slowest/worst-case scenario? In the above example, Marcy will reach her FI number at sixty-five years old, as long as she can invest $4,800 a year (or $400 a month). She doesn't get to reach FI in her initial ten-year time frame but at least now she knows what she'd have to do in order to get there. This is still incorporating her lifestyle goals and other goals. If she's able to earn more or find even more room in her gap, she can have her time to reach FI cut down significantly. But if she takes more time to begin to invest and increase her gap, Scenario 4, then she will have $270,000 by sixty-five years old.

- If you are not okay with your current baseline timeline, what are you willing to change?

- How much will you spend or need in the future so that you can reduce your FI number (adjusting your Guac lifestyle level)?

- How much will you earn on the path so that you have more to invest and reach other goals?

- How much longer are you willing to work to balance your desired Guac lifestyle levels and financial goals?

If you're not happy with the forecasted timeline and you're not willing to work on the components of the FI formula, then you'll need to make peace with your current timeline and enjoy the journey.

This is why finding work you love and enjoying it on the path is so important. While one of the main goals of this FI journey is to set you up so you don't have to work forever—or so you have the flexibility to choose the work you do and how much you work—the process will put you in a position where you'll be more content and experience varying levels of financial freedom while on your path.

Now that you have an estimated timeline for reaching FI, remember that this is just a starting point. You'll be able to modify this timeline in accordance with the strategies you acquire and implement from Part 3. Once you have integrated the new strategies, revisit the exercise and make necessary adjustments to the timeline. For access to resources and spreadsheets to help you map out your FI plan, go to www.yourjourneytofinancialfreedom.com.

Part 2: Creating Your Enjoyable Financial Independence Plan Checklist

☐ Assess Your Current Mindset & Habits

☐ Uncover The Desired Guac Level You Want To Live Now & in FI

☐ Identify Your Lifestyle Goals

☐ Organize & Prioritize Your Financial Goals

☐ Know Your Current Numbers (Income, Expenses, Assets & Liabilities)

☐ Forecast Your Future Numbers (FI #, Income, Expenses, Assets & Liabilities)

☐ Create A Budget That Includes Your Financial Goals & Lifestyle Goals

☐ Map Out Different Scenarios of How Long It Will Take You To Reach Your FI Goals

PART 3:

EXECUTING YOUR PLAN

Congratulations, by following the steps in the previous chapters, you've created your initial FI plan! You should now have an idea of your FI number, your starting point, and the estimated time frame it will take you.

Parts 1 and 2 of this book were all about understanding what FI is, what it takes to reach FI, defining your goals, and planning your journey to FI. This section, Part 3, is all about taking action and implementing the necessary adjustments to reach FI plus your other financial and lifestyle goals. Therefore, the next four chapters are dedicated to showing you how you can:

- Optimize Your Expenses

- Increase Your Income

- Pay Down Your Liabilities

- Increase Your Assets

Since the following chapters are all about taking action, let's spend a quick moment addressing the emotional and mental challenges that may come up for you as you begin to implement these changes.

The emotional and mental effort needed to make the necessary adjustments to the different parts of the FI formula—income, expenses, assets and liabilities—will vary not just based on your external circumstances but your inner circumstances, like your personality and preferences (all which are an extension of your mindset and habits).

For example, my friend Denise seems to handle big changes like moving to different states or switching companies seamlessly, although, I have no doubt it still takes consideration and effort on her part to follow through on the big decisions she makes. Denise will leave a job in a heartbeat if she is presented with a better opportunity. She is always prepared to interview for another job, even if she's happy in her current position. Because of that, Denise was able to increase her income from $55,000 to over $200,000 in the span of fifteen years.

Denise is open to swift and big changes that have had a dramatic positive impact on her income and overall finances. What she seems to do with ease, scares the hell out of me. Even with my "click on the hyperlink" mindset and can-do attitude, making those types of big changes that seemingly come so easily to Denise are harder for me. I stayed at my corporate job for thirteen years, even as my commute became insufferable. I could have gotten a job somewhere closer to home, but the thought of such a big change scared me. I love stability and consistency. I like knowing what to expect from my environment, so moving to another city or thinking about changing jobs is a higher emotional and mental hurdle for me to leap over. It's not that I can't do it—it just takes a lot more effort. Unless I view the change as necessary, I'll put it off for as long as I can. Knowing this about myself and figuring out my tolerance level for change helps me set realistic expectations for how I optimize parts of my FI formula.

Knowing how you deal with change will be important for you to figure out the adjustments you'll make to the various FI formula components. Even though you'll hear advice from personal finance experts telling you to do things like switch careers, move to another city, or sell your home and downsize, the mental and emotional effort to make these big changes—even if they'd help you tremendously on your financial journey—can be difficult to make.

Changes that require the most emotional and mental effort like leaving a job you're comfortable in or selling the home you love also tend to have the biggest impact on your money. Even so, what may seem like a small adjustment to one person, such as giving up daily coffee purchases, can be just as emotionally and mentally challenging as a larger adjustment. The daily decisions we make about ongoing expenses and habits require constant effort to be consistent, until new habits and ways of life form.

When even thinking about making changes in your life, it's normal to feel overwhelmed. However, it's important to recognize that this feeling can be a chance to do something different and an opportunity for growth. Even though it might seem easier to take the path of avoidance or inaction, to achieve different results and live the life you desire, you'll need to work through the fear and complacency to take action. This may be challenging, but it's an essential part of the process of creating positive change in your life and your FI journey.

9

OPTIMIZE EXPENSES

We already looked at your expenses in Chapter 8 to see how much you're truly spending. If you skipped that exercise, now is your chance to go and complete it because you can't optimize your expenses, cut down on what's holding you back, or spend more on what can help you without knowing what they are.

Many of us, especially when first starting on this conscious financial journey, may have been previously oblivious to the way we spend our money on a regular basis, which can leave room for mindless or wasteful spending. It's why most financial experts advise cutting back on your expenses as a starting point. According to a survey, Americans spend an average of $1,497 per month or $18,000 a year on nonessential items like eating out, cable and streaming services, subscription boxes, and other superfluous spending. Optimizing our expenses, or eliminating waste in the way we spend is a great way to see some quick wins with our money.

If you can find a few hundred dollars to cut out of your budget by simply canceling something you don't need or use, or changing a behavior like how often you go out to eat, you can no doubt find a way to increase your gap and save more money. But the key word is *simply*. Just because something seems simple doesn't mean it's easy. It's often not easy to change the habits or things we find comforting even if that comfort is holding us back from being able to reach our goals. It's why we first talked about working on improving your mindset and habits earlier in the book to give you the internal momentum needed to follow through on the external behaviors that will help you get the money outcomes you want to achieve.

While in this chapter we will be focusing on looking at your expenses, the goal here isn't to minimize your expenses or make them the lowest they can possibly be (unless you want them to be that way). But we will also talk about ways in which you can increase your spending in areas that you see fit. Remember this is your journey and your choice.

If you are living at the poverty line, only making minimum wage or even middle-income wages but have kids, dependents, and other financial responsibilities, then the advice on cutting back most likely won't apply to you. You're more than likely doing the best you can with the little that you have. You'll need to focus on increasing your income while being financially responsible so that you can make progress. Even so, doing this exercise to examine your expenses can't hurt because you'll know that you've done your due diligence in working on this component to the best of your ability. Yet still, for many, there may be ways to save $100 to $500 per month right now with small changes that can go a long way toward reaching the goals they've identified.

Assessing your expenses is helpful regardless of how much you make, because it shows you where your money is going. This is also a starting point to see opportunities to increase spending in areas that will provide more security, comfort, and joy in your life once you start making more money. A budget doesn't necessarily have to be solely used for reducing expenses; it can also assist in identifying areas where you can afford to spend more. Now isn't that exciting?

I don't want you to completely and indefinitely cut out the things that matter to you and give your life joy. But you may need to do that temporarily. I'm asking you to take an honest look at what you spend your money on and then make a conscious choice of whether it is worth the additional time and money it takes to pay for that expense.

EVALUATE EXPENSES BASED ON YOUR JOURNEYER STAGE AND GUAC LEVEL

Depending on your Journeyer stage and desired Guac level lifestyle, you may have to put more effort into trimming back expenses until you're able to get to a better or stronger position on your journey. If you are an Explorer or Cadet and working on stability and paying off debt, you'll need to be more aggressive with optimizing your expenses so that you can get out of those stages as quickly as possible relative to your level of comfort. When it comes to the level of aggressiveness and speed at which you are willing to put effort to get through each stage of the journey, it will depend on your desired Guacamole lifestyle level—not the one you are living now but what kind of lifestyle you want to ultimately have. You may be trying to live a Guac 3 or 4 lifestyle now and can't really afford to, which is putting your financial future and probability of reaching FI at risk. Knowing your desired Guac lifestyle level will help you determine how uncomfortable you're willing to feel as you begin to scale back on your expenses. If you truly are happy with a Guac level 1 or 2, a simpler life that doesn't involve excessive spending, then making some of these changes may not be as tough. But if you truly desire a higher Guac level lifestyle in all areas of your life, then cutting back on expenses may feel harder for you.

Josie, a listener of the podcast and guest on episode 113, was constantly spending her money as she made it. It wasn't until a vacation where she came back with all her credit cards maxed out and no savings that she realized she needed to change. She started by selling her excess name-brand belongings, and this led to her adopting a minimalist lifestyle. By cutting back and becoming more conscious of her spending habits, she was able to pay off $50,000 of debt and focus on investing, moving from the Cadet stage to the Aviator stage by adjusting her Guac lifestyle level to hit her goals.

If you are living and also desire to live a more expensive or luxurious Guacamole lifestyle, let's say Guac 3, 4, or 5, then making these changes to your expenses may feel a little more uncomfortable and there may be some friction in this. That's why it's important to identify your current Journeyer stage and your desired Guac level to help set expectations for yourself as you work through the expense and income side of the formula.

Once upon a time, I thought I *needed* the luxury items

and expensive things I bought, regardless of the cost. It felt like I was doing myself a disservice by not "having the best" because I worked hard and I believed I was entitled to it. Besides, others around me seemed to be living a luxurious life, at least on the surface. Why didn't I deserve the same lifestyle? I worked hard and made decent money, so why shouldn't I have "nice things"?

I wasted a lot of money treating myself to things I thought I needed, but that was before I knew about or understood the goal of FI. It wasn't that I didn't deserve a nice car, but I bought it in my Cadet stage while working a job I didn't like, not realizing that spending over $30,000 on a car only increased the time it would take for me to either leave my job or progress to the next Journeyer level.

Currently, I'm in the Commander stage, where I'm considering the idea of purchasing a newer and more luxurious car. However, before making any decisions, I'll evaluate whether spending that amount of money is worth extending the length of time I'll need to work to recover financially, or worth increasing my monthly expenses. While it's true that I can afford it, I'm still carefully weighing the potential trade-offs. By being aware of the total costs associated with this purchase, I feel more empowered to make a decision that aligns with my financial goals and journey.

If you are struggling to swim and keep afloat because of a costly expense, you may want to cut off whatever is weighing you down. Your emotional and mental connection to that expense can keep you holding on to it longer than you need to, which makes it take longer than necessary to reach your destination, or worse, puts you at risk of sinking. Imagine being able to know you can cut that line and circle back for it when you have more strength (are in a better financial position). Some connections and tethers aren't just emotional and mental connections—they are legit obligations and responsibilities you have to take care of like covering rent or childcare. This is why paying off consumer debt in the Cadet stage is so crucial, as is understanding the difference between your mandatory expenses and discretionary expenses. Having fewer tethers or sandbags in the form of expenses, attached to you while you get out of the earlier Journeyer stages allows you to move forward with less effort and struggle. But you must have the mindset and willingness to release what's holding you back.

WHEN EXPENSES ARE SELF-NURTURING INVESTMENTS

Expenses when looked at differently can be a form of an investment into the quality of your life. For example, paying for a gym membership is an expense but can be an investment in your physical health as long as you actually use the membership and feel like it's an important part of your lifestyle. It's especially an investment when it also contributes positively to other parts of your FI formula—e.g., going to the gym is a positive habit that helps you mentally and emotionally. It's your "you" time and a way to get the serotonin going in your body, which in turn gives you more confidence and energy at work, which directly impacts how you're viewed by your boss and peers, potentially helping you get picked for more projects or opportunities to make money.

If investing in a gym membership is beneficial to you because you have no desire to exercise at home, the monthly expense yields greater advantages compared to eliminating it and allocating the funds towards your savings or investing.

Let's do the math on that. For example, if you spent $69 a month on a gym membership, you'd spend $828 per year or $8,280 over ten years. If you were to invest that money instead, assuming an 8% return rate and $100 starting balance, you'd have $12,845 at the end of the ten years. As long as you're using it, the gym membership is more valuable in a way that can't be measured and will undoubtedly help with your mindset and habits. The potential benefits you gain far surpass whatever money you saved or accumulated through investing from not having a membership or the $12,845 you might gain from investing that money.

Remember, you don't need to eliminate every expense or view this process solely based on numbers. Determine what you don't value or utilize and identify your genuine priorities.

While I'm giving you full permission to look at spending money in ways that increase the quality of your life and I agree that certain expenses can be an investment, don't fall into the trap of justifying harmful spending habits that keep you stuck on your financial independence journey.

IMPROVING MINDSET AND HABITS AROUND YOUR EXPENSES

When it comes to managing your expenses, it's not just about creating a budget and cutting back on spending. It's also important to examine your mindset and thoughts around your spending. By reframing the way you look at things, you can shift from a mindset of deprivation and sacrifice to one of empowerment and abundance. For example, instead of feeling like you have to pay for something, try shifting your perspective to one of gratitude that you get to pay for it. Similarly, rather than feeling like you are depriving yourself of something you want, try seeing it as taking care of yourself and prioritizing your financial goals. By working on your mindset and thought patterns around money, you can improve your relationship with finances and make more informed decisions about your expenses.

As we discussed before, developing positive habits can have a significant impact on your expenses. The example of waking up late can show how a habit can lead to a rushed morning routine and force you to buy breakfast and lunch, even if it is not your preferred choice of food. This habit can quickly add up and cost you money over time. However, by cultivating the positive habit of going to bed at a reasonable hour, you can give yourself enough time in the morning to prepare breakfast and lunch at home.

To see how this looks in the real world, let's look at the examples of Liz and Jazmine:

Liz always goes to bed late and is unable to get up in the morning. She knows she wants to save more money and start investing but doesn't feel like she has anything left over at the end of the month. She's always in a rush in the mornings going to work and never has time to make breakfast or pack lunch so she stops and picks up her bagel and coffee for $5 every morning and ends up ordering lunch out with her coworkers and spends $15. She spends about $20 a day on breakfast and lunch which amounts to $400 a month.

Jazmine is also in debt and wants to find ways to pay it off faster. Just like Liz, she has had the past habit of waking up late and not having enough time to make her own breakfast or bring lunch. She knows it's not the best habit so she decides she will try to get a good night's rest so she can get up with enough time to eat breakfast before she leaves for work and packs her lunch the night before. She intentionally knows what days she will order lunch with her coworkers and leaves room for flexibility in case something comes up. Because she eats breakfast at home and only buys lunch once or twice a week, she spends about $160 a month and is able to put an additional $240 toward her debt payoff goals.

Creating the positive habit of going to bed earlier allows you to get up and prep your breakfast and lunch at home. You can consciously decide if you want to eat out or make your own food allowing you to control the way you spend your money.

THE BENEFIT OF BEING ON A NAIL

When it comes to achieving your financial goals, the level of intensity and determination is up to you. Some goals may be tied to an emotional point that you want to reach as quickly as possible. In these cases, you may find it valuable to increase your intensity and make short-term sacrifices in order to reach your goal more quickly. I really disliked my commute and job when I was working in corporate so stumbling upon this concept of financial independence and feeling like it was my only realistic way out of my situation really lit a fire in me. I was willing to be intense for the first couple of years because of the discomfort I felt in my current situation.

It reminds me of a story by motivational speaker and author

Les Brown, where he tells the tale of a passerby who walked by a man with a whimpering dog on a porch. The passerby asked the man what was wrong with the dog, and the man said, "He's laying on a nail." The man walking by was shocked and asked, "Why doesn't your dog just get up?" The owner said, "Because it's not hurting bad enough for him to get up."

Is there something about your life that is displeasing to you that can be directly correlated to your finances, because of a lack of money?

"I don't like my job, but I can't quit because…I have no money saved up."

"I want to move out of my parents' house but can't because I don't have enough money."

"I want to take more time to travel but don't have the money."

"I know I need to invest but can't find extra money."

That displeased and unsatisfied feeling is the nail. In my case the nail causing me discomfort was my job and commute. That nail hurt for a long time but apparently not enough for me to do anything about it until I could no longer ignore it. Once I began having kids, being on that nail was unbearable and growing my family and adding more to my plate exacerbated the pain. I *had* to get up. And by getting up, it meant changing anything I needed to reach the goal of being able to one day quit and reach financial independence. For me that meant budgeting and prioritizing saving and investing over discretionary expenses like vacations, shopping, or going out to eat. Once I was able to leave my job my intensity for wanting to save and invest aggressively was tempered. While we still save and invest because of where we are currently in the journey, I can focus more on how I can enjoy and spend now in a way that will make my family's and my life comfortable. This comes with the trade-off of having less money at the end of my life because I'm spending more now and choosing not to invest it. I'm able to balance the long term and the short term partly because I don't have the discomfort of being in a job I don't like or a long commute. I'm comfortable with where I am on the financial journey (Journeyer stage) *and* with the quality of my day-to-day life (Guacamole level). While being comfortable is the actual goal, it can impact your willingness to sacrifice or do something drastic to change your situation.

If you are currently uncomfortable with the debt you're in, or are in a job or relationship you don't like or that's not emotionally/physically/mentally safe but are staying because of financial reasons, then looking at ways to cut your expenses so that you can leave is not something that should feel restrictive but rather is the key to your liberation. The unsatisfied and uncomfortable feeling with your current situation may not seem like an advantage, but it is. It can give you the energy, motivation, and momentum you need to make the necessary change.

UNDERSPENDING CAN BE A PROBLEM TOO

Although it's important to optimize your spending and cut back if necessary to achieve your financial goals, it's also possible to go overboard with analyzing your expenses. This can lead to underspending, excessive overthinking, and wasting time and energy, or missing out on valuable experiences due to unnecessary stress. I sometimes still catch myself overthinking small spending decisions. This happened during my mother's sixtieth birthday trip to Portugal when I didn't want to miss an episode of the popular show, *House of the Dragon*, which was not available on my expired HBO subscription. The alternative was to add HBO to my cable account and pay for a VPN service for $30. Rather than simply paying to watch it, I spent hours searching for a free solution, wasting valuable time and energy on my vacation. Once I came to my senses and paid the $30 to be able to watch the show, I reflected back on how easy it is to get caught up in optimizing for just saving money and not thinking about what we are losing or giving up by being so frugal.

I had a friend who was deliberating whether to visit our mutual friend for Thanksgiving, but the flight ticket cost $100 more than usual due to the holiday season. She was about to cancel the trip and spend the holiday alone instead. I suggested that she consider the value of spending time with close friends on a holiday rather than saving the extra $100, which she would typically spend on two brunches or one bottomless brunch in NYC anyway. After thinking it through, she realized that being with loved ones on a holiday when she didn't want to be alone was worth more than saving $100. She booked the ticket and had the best time with her friends.

When we're looking at spending in a way that makes us want to cut back, we can sometimes miss out on the real purposes for having money. Not only to save and invest but to also spend in a way that provides convenience and comfort. If you have the money to spend in ways that bring you joy, you should.

The Inequity of Keeping Up with the Joneses

For individuals from marginalized groups, particularly Black people who have historically been excluded from opportunities to build wealth such as home ownership, there are both systemic and psychological reasons for our desire to spend money on visible status symbols. In a society where you may feel overlooked and undervalued, showing your value through material and external things has been a way to prove worth and establish status.

Researchers studied data collected from 1986 to 2002 for the Consumer Expenditure Survey conducted by the federal Bureau of Labor Statistics found that Blacks and Hispanics spend up to 30% more than whites of comparable income on visible goods like clothing, cars, and jewelry. This meant that, compared to white households of similar income, the typical Black and Hispanic household spent $2,300 more per year on visible items. To do that, they spent less on almost all other categories except housing, and they saved less.

If you were raised in a family where you lived paycheck to paycheck or in poverty where there was little left over to spend on the "nice to haves" you may feel more compelled to spend money on your own terms in an unrestrictive way. It's also important to acknowledge that the wealth gap in the US for Black individuals is significant, as highlighted by the Pew Research Center's 2020 study which found that Black households have a median net worth of $24,100, which is only 13% of the median net worth of white households ($188,200).

We all have different starting points and reasons for why it may take us longer to overcome more internal and external obstacles to reach some of our goals. If you view material items as a priority or have tended to prioritize lifestyle goals over financial goals, that doesn't make you wrong or a bad person. It could very well be a legitimate form of taste preference, but it can also be an attempt to prove your value to others. Being aware of this and your motivation on why you spend or want to spend the way you do is important. If luxury items are what you desire, then you should have them but not at the complete expense of your current and future financial security.

WAYS TO SAVE ON EXPENSE CATEGORIES

When it comes to cutting back on expenses, some experts say it's easier to focus on the discretionary expenses, but you can find ways to cut back on mandatory expenses too. Just because an expense is mandatory and a must-have doesn't mean you can't find ways to save money in that category. Reexamining your mandatory expenses, which are typically the highest expenditures in your budget, can often result in finding a bigger gap. By taking a closer look at these expenses, you can explore alternative options to reduce your costs without sacrificing quality. In this context, we will discuss some practical ways to save money on your mandatory expenses and some discretionary expenses.

Housing

Your housing is a mandatory fixed expense whether you rent or buy. Your rent or mortgage (principal and interest) typically stays the same and is usually your biggest expense. While this is not just a category you can completely cut out—unless you have amazing parents or family that allow you to move in with them free—you can begin to rethink ways to save on this expense. If you own, you may find that your mortgage is just too high in comparison to your income. The biggest and most drastic thing you can do is sell your house and relocate to a smaller home or more inexpensive area. This of course depends on your willingness to make such a big change, the real estate market, your attachment to your home, your job, and more. For some people, making a big decision like this feels possible and for others this is not even up for discussion. You can also consider house hacking which involves having a multiunit property and renting out a unit so that a tenant helps pay the mortgage. Also, taking on a roommate if you have the space can off set your housing costs.

Groceries

When it comes to saving on groceries, a little planning can go a long way. One of the simplest and most effective ways to save on your grocery bill is to make a list before heading to the store. This can help you stick to your budget and avoid impulse purchases. Additionally, keep an eye out for coupons and deals on the items you need. Consider buying generic or store-brand items, which are often less expensive than brand-name products. Finally, be flexible with your meal planning and shop based on what's on sale or in season.

Monthly Bills

With monthly bills, everything can be negotiated. Taking the time to call your providers to ask for discounts or negotiate better deals can save you hundreds a month. Set time aside on your calendar to make these calls and reward yourself after completing each one. The reward can be simple, like your favorite candy or beverage.

Navigating Outings with Family and Friends

The feelings and opinions of others can make it difficult to stick to a budget, especially with social events and outings. Even if you are in debt or trying to save money, it's important to find a balance between your financial goals and your desire to have fun with friends and family. It's unrealistic to think that just because you're in debt or not where you want to be financially, you can ignore the value of connecting with family and friends, whether it's them wanting to celebrate something with you or your own desire to go out and have fun. Sure it may be easy to turn down acquaintances or people you don't really want to hang out with, but what about navigating those times when you do want to go and hang out? There will be some people who can stop seeing friends and family cold turkey and stick to their spending boundaries, declining all invitations to happy hour or dinners out with friends that don't fall into a preplanned budget. And there are people like me who need to feel free when it comes to spending money, who want the ability to be impulsive without adhering to a strict budget.

When creating your budget, be practical and set aside money for activities like dining out or having fun. It's unreasonable to expect that you'll suddenly start spending only $20 after previously spending $500 on brunches and bars, and I'm not suggesting you try to do so. It's better to gradually allocate a smaller budget of $300 or $350 instead and be realistic about what you're able to do.

In some cases, there may be expenses that you can't escape or reduce. Tracy from episode 296 of the podcast and her wife were able to pay off $170,000 of debt in ten years by making conscious choices to prioritize debt repayment by living frugally and refraining from expensive vacations or major purchases. Despite their focus on debt repayment, they also continued to contribute a modest amount to their retirement accounts and stayed focused on their goals. Tracy also shared what makes her financial journey unique as a member of the LGBTQ+ community and the importance of acknowledging the financial concerns that queer individuals face. When Tracy and her wife had their child, they had to go through a second-parent adoption process, even though Tracy is the biological parent. This process incurred significant financial costs that opposite sex couples using donor sperm typically don't experience. Expenses such as gender-affirming health care and legal name changes can be substantial and not always covered by insurance. The costs and difficulties faced can vary depending on where one resides, as some states have enacted discriminatory laws targeting LGBTQ+ individuals, which can impact their ability to choose affordable places to live. Despite these challenges, Tracy emphasizes the importance of seeking out local resources for networking and support, such as the National LGBT Chamber of Commerce, and legal organizations and health care centers that cater specifically to the needs of the LGBTQ+ community.

FOUR QUESTIONS TO HELP YOU EVALUATE EXPENSES

In order to gain insight into your current expenses, you can examine each one and ask four key questions:

- What is the value and/or joy of this expense to you from 1 to 5 (1 = high value/joy, 5 = low value/joy)?

- Can you decrease the expense? Yes or no.

- If you answered yes to question 2, what can/will you do? If no, why not?

- Does this expense take you closer or further away from your life and financial goals?

There will be some expenses that are easy to let go of and cut out of your budget because they bring you low value/joy or can just be optimized better. That's what makes us unique. Don't judge yourself for your initial responses but be honest about where you stand and how you feel about the expenses in your life.

You can assess where you are with your expenses based on the four questions to see if each expense is something you want to keep as is, can cut out completely, or cut back to help you create more room in your gap.

This exercise is not meant to make you cut everything out or back. This is not an act of making your life smaller—this is a way to expand your life by intentionally spending in a way that matters to you.

If you are combining your finances with a partner and on the journey to FI together, this process will undoubtedly look different—after all you might not value the same things. Instead of just thinking about what matters to you and what you can do, you'll need to find out where your partner stands on these questions and find common ground if your answers are different. I recommend having each partner answer the questions separately and then come together to go over each other's responses. This will help you to understand what motivates or is important to the other person. It can also explain why if you've tried to get on a budget in the past it may have been hard to get the other person on board. Maybe their top joy spending item is your least important, or maybe they don't want to change or reduce something and you do. Having the answers is a good starting point with your partner so you can work together to create more gaps by optimizing your expenses.

For example, let's say that you go through all of your expenses and decide that you are not willing to cut anything out or back. While it is true that you can focus solely on expanding your income to create the gap you need, you can't outearn senseless or unconscious spending habits. It's one thing to go through the expenses you have and legitimately not see any room to cut back or cut out, but you may surprise yourself while doing this exercise as most people can find ways to cut back on things that don't matter to them as much as reaching the goals you've set for yourself.

I often experience this when I'm deciding to have a mojito or other sugary drink. As superficial as it sounds, I'd like a tighter midsection, but in order to achieve that long-term goal, I'll need to make sacrifices now like cutting out certain foods that make me bloat like carbs and sugary drinks. At that moment, sometimes I care more about enjoying that drink or meal instead of getting abs and so I choose the drink. I'm fine with the balanced approach I take now to achieving my fitness goals and my current outcome.

This same mentality can be applied to your financial journey. You may find yourself thinking, *I could allocate more funds toward saving or investing, but it may require giving up some of the things I currently enjoy, which I find worthwhile.* Your personal choice involves finding your "enough points," which represent the level at which you are content with the balance between your present situation and the cost it may incur in the future. This choice also involves determining the level of intensity at which you wish to pursue your goals. You may choose to go all in and cut every unnecessary thing out of your budget for a few years and live a more Guac 1 or 2 lifestyle to achieve your goals in order to live the life of freedom you want a few years down the road. You may actually enjoy the simplicity of frugal living and decide that the Guac 1 or 2 lifestyle is permanent. Or you may decide that you are not willing to compromise too much and want to live that Guac 3-plus lifestyle now, which may mean it takes you longer to reach your goals or you need to adjust your goals. What you do now matters to what happens later. Reducing expenses in certain areas is not only about saving a few dollars—it's also about developing discipline and changing behavior that may be more out of habit and reactive than intentional action. So while this exercise of cutting back or cutting out things from your budget may seem mundane it can make a big difference in the quality of your lifestyle and the amount of time it takes you to reach your ultimate version of financial independence.

10

INCREASE INCOME

Your income is a critical factor in your ability to reach FI. Without income you can't pay for your expenses or have a gap that helps you accomplish anything else you want to do like invest, save, buy a house, travel, etc. Ultimately, from the more than two hundred interviews I've done on the *JTL* podcast, talking to people who have made extraordinary progress toward their FI goals, income was the driving force. While cutting a couple hundred dollars from your expenses is a good start, unless you're naturally geared toward a simple, frugal lifestyle, doubling your income or earning thousands more will have the biggest impact. Even with making more money, you'll need to be thoughtful with your expenses because even a millionaire can run out of money if they're not careful.

Previously, we talked about the four purposes for your income: pay for mandatory expenses, pay down liabilities, buy more assets, and pay for discretionary expenses. Two of those purposes—paying down liabilities and buying more assets—

help you move through the five Journeyer stages to FI and the other two purposes—paying for mandatory and discretionary expenses—are more related to the Guacamole level you want to live. The more of your income that you apply toward your assets and liabilities, the faster you can go through the Journeyer stages and cover your short- and long-term financial goals. The amount of income that you apply toward mandatory and discretionary expenses determines how well you can enjoy your lifestyle today.

For example, if you decide to put more or most of your gap toward your annual vacation fund rather than investing it in your retirement accounts, you'll have less money in your retirement account but the ability to take the vacation you want. This happened to me as I was writing this part of the book. My tax preparer wrote to me to see if I wanted to contribute additional money to my retirement account before the close of tax season. He crunched the numbers and said the maximum I could contribute was $27,000. If I made the full allowable contribution it would increase our tax refund by $7,000 and put more money into investments to help hit our FI goals. I had a moment of pause to think through what I should do. My first thought was that this was the smart financial decision and that I should find a way to make it work. Then I thought about all of the more lifestyle-related goals we had in the coming years—like buying a new car, fixing our backyard, and taking our first trip to Disney World—and knew that the money would be better spent on these quality of life purchases. Besides, we are already on track to hit our FI goals and while being able to reach FI sooner would be nice, it's not as important as en-joying our money today.

Because this book is about enjoying the journey while on the path to financial independence, I'll guide you on how to split your income so that you can have the best of both worlds—to have your cake (financial independence) and to eat it too (enjoy the benefits of financial independence while on the journey, having financial freedom). What's the point of baking the cake and reaching your financial goals if you can't enjoy the process, taking the occasional lick from the mixing spoon, or my favorite, eating the leftover icing like my mom let me have. You'll need enough icing and cake to go around which means you'll need enough income to sat-isfy your lifestyle and financial goals.

It's simple: the more money you make and keep to invest and save, the faster you'll be able to achieve financial inde-pendence and security. But you'll need enough income in order to satisfy your desired Guacamole lifestyle level (pay-ing for your current lifestyle desires) and to help you move through the Journeyer stages in order to make this journey enjoyable and successful.

A HIGH SALARY WON'T FIX EVERYTHING

Having a high salary alone won't remove every roadblock and erase your problems. You still need to be a good steward of the income that flows in to be able to use it in a way that not only serves you to live well today but serves you in the future too. A lot of white-collar professions offer six-figure salaries, but they also come with six-figure student loan debts.

I've heard this a lot in my podcast interviews with lawyers and doctors. I'd also like to note that not all lawyers earn six figures. Although the journey to freedom from debt and progressing through the stages of the financial journey will differ for six-figure earners compared to those who earn lower- to mid-tier salaries, it still requires hard work and changes in habits to make progress.

Many high earners are only income rich and not balance sheet rich, also known as HENRYs—High Earners Not Rich Yet—a term created by Shawn Tully in a 2003 *Fortune* magazine article. It referred to people earning six figures and more, but who were not able to convert their high income into owning assets. Their cash flow relied solely on working for money in exchange for their time and energy. Once you stop working or can't work, you have no money, but you need to pay for your expenses, which forces you to keep working, even if you'd prefer to retire. The key is to shift from relying solely on active cash income to acquiring and owning assets that appreciate in value over time. This approach allows your passive income to gradually accumulate and eventually cover your living expenses.

Attaining complete FI or a level of it, often requires a relatively high income, which is why reaching FI is often considered a privilege. Living frugally while having a high income is totally different from having a low income and having no choice but to spend frugally. You have the liberty and the ability to decide how to use your money, when you have enough of it. You're making spending choices from a place of power and abundance vs. constraint. If an unexpected financial emergency arises or you wish to alter your Guacamole lifestyle, you can because you have the financial resources and flexibility to make a different decision.

In order to achieve your desired lifestyle and financial goals, you need to earn significantly more than a basic living wage that can pay for your current expenses and allow you to invest and build a portfolio that can provide you with sufficient income. The federal minimum wage as of 2023 in the United States is $7.25 per hour, which translates to an annual salary of $15,000 for full-time work at forty hours per week. The federal poverty threshold for a single person in 2022 is set at $13,590, and $27,750 for a family of four. While some FI enthusiasts may choose to live at or below the poverty line, many others have no choice but to do so, and face the struggle and hardship that come along with it.

If you are making minimum wage or earn a lower income, I want to acknowledge that your journey may take longer and you'll have to give yourself grace. If you are able to keep your spending low and are content with a more modest lifestyle, you may still be able to reach your financial goals, even with a lower income. But, having a lower income and a desire to maintain a more expensive lifestyle can make it more challenging to reach your financial goals, unless you work on increasing your income.

It's also critical to recognize the income gap between Black and Latino communities and the white community, especially when discussing FI. As of 2021, the US Census Bureau reports that the median household income for Black families was $48,400, compared to $76,000 for white families. Similarly, the median household income for Hispanic families was $63,500, lower than that of white families. Additionally, Native American and Indigenous communities also face significant economic disparities. These income disparities stem from systemic factors such as historic and ongoing discrimination, unequal access to quality education, limited employment opportunities, and institutionalized racism.

I mention this not to discourage you if you fall into one of these minority groups with lower incomes, but to acknowledge that there are external factors that are beyond our control. However, these realities emphasize the importance of increasing our income and building wealth.

Now we will discuss various ways to increase your income, starting with maximizing your earning potential in your current job, followed by exploring other job opportunities, and finally, we'll discuss how to create your own income-producing opportunities by capitalizing on your skills and expertise. By implementing some of these strategies, you'll be able to increase your income and work toward your financial goals.

INCREASE YOUR INCOME AT YOUR CURRENT JOB

If you're looking to increase your income, one of the first places to start is with your current job. There may be untapped opportunities for growth and advancement that could lead to a higher salary or benefits.

Here are just a few ways you can maximize your earning potential at your current job:

- Ask for more money right now.

- Do more/better work, negotiate more money in the future.

- Do overtime or take on more paid opportunities.

- Switch positions/roles within the company.

- Upgrade your skills and education to become more valuable to your current employer.

- Seek out promotions and opportunities for advancement within the company.

- Negotiate for additional benefits, such as better health care, retirement plans, or more vacation time.

- Look for opportunities to earn commissions or bonuses in addition to your base salary.

- Explore options for remote work or flexible scheduling, which could potentially increase your income by allowing you to take on additional work or side hustles.

- Network within your industry to build relationships and potentially open up new job opportunities with higher salaries or better benefits.

- Move to a new company.

I've chosen a few of these strategies to explain in detail below.

Ask for More Money Right Now

If you are a reliable and valuable employee, it's possible to increase your income without putting in additional effort. One way to achieve this is by requesting a raise from your employer, who hopefully appreciates your hard work and dedication and may be willing to offer you more money. It's crucial to keep in mind that the worst that can happen is that your employer says no, but at least you have demonstrated your ambition and desire to receive fair compensation. By asking for a raise, you put yourself on the radar of decision-makers when budgets and promotions are being considered. If your employer cannot provide the salary you deserve, it may be time to explore other opportunities.

Do More/Better Work, Negotiate More Money in the Future

On the other hand, it's important to be honest with yourself if you're not performing at your best in your current job. Your goal should be to give your best effort and enjoy your job, not just to please your employer but also yourself. When you work in the zone and project positive energy, you'll open yourself up to more opportunities and develop skills that can be applied beyond your current job. For instance, you can set a two-week experiment to give your best at work, such as speaking up more during meetings, contributing new ideas to management, or assisting colleagues. Pay attention to how your thoughts and energy change internally and whether others around you take notice.

It's unlikely that you will receive an immediate raise after two weeks of amazing work, but your improved energy may lead to management taking notice. Even if they don't, the experience and skills gained from performing well will be invaluable for future job opportunities. By consistently performing well over time, you'll be better positioned to ask for a raise or apply for a better job when the opportunity arises.

Do Overtime or Take On More Paid Opportunities

Are you at a job that allows you to work overtime or offers you other ways that you can supplement your income? If so, take advantage of those additional earning opportunities if your schedule allows for it. For example, if you're a teacher you may be able to supplement your income through taking on more teaching periods, tutoring, coaching sport teams, and working summer school.

Earning more money from overtime and extra jobs will allow you to pay off debt, fund your low-cost side hustle, and/or invest more. These extra jobs can just be temporary until you satisfy a financial goal or get to a Journeyer stage you find comfortable.

LOOK INTO JOB OPPORTUNITIES AT OTHER COMPANIES

Exploring job opportunities outside of your current company is a proactive way to increase your income. One advantage of switching companies is that new employees often receive higher salaries, bonuses, and perks. Even if your current company offers small annual salary increases, you may still be earning less than a new hire with similar skills and experience. Updating your LinkedIn profile and résumé is crucial in preparing for potential job opportunities. Make sure to highlight your current work experience and responsibilities to showcase your skills and qualifications to potential employers. Additionally, networking and reaching out to industry connections can be helpful in finding new job opportunities. Keep in mind that switching jobs can also offer new challenges and opportunities for growth and career advancement. However, it's important to weigh the pros and cons of leaving your current job before making any decisions.

Whether you're planning to stay at your current job or looking for opportunities elsewhere, you will need to make allies and have connections with people who can speak your name in rooms where you want to be. The saying that *your network is your net worth* is absolutely true. Most of the positions or open roles are filled before they are even publicly posted because someone was in mind already for that role or recommended by a friend of someone with influence. If you don't have influence or connections, you'll have to create them for yourself. Create a list of people you'd like to network with in your job, such as upper management or peers who have distinguished themselves as standouts or who are in a position you want to eventually move into. Send an email or LinkedIn message introducing yourself and explain how you would love to treat them to coffee for fifteen to thirty minutes of their time to learn more about their role and their experience at their job. These are called informational interviews because you are not interviewing for a job or asking for anything other than information. People love those who take initiative and people also love to talk about themselves. This allows you to begin to not only make the connections but learn more about said role.

During these informational interviews, you can ask about their experience at the firm, such as opportunities, work-life balance, assignments, etc., and get a sense of the company culture and how it aligns with your own work style. It's also important to note that it's not always about getting a job offer, but instead getting more information and building professional connections. The key is to be persistent and remember that you only need one yes to get the opportunity to have the conversation and learn more.

Norly, a guest on episode 278 of the podcast, was motivated to secure a higher-paying job to pay off her six-figure student law degree loans. Her current job was not paying her enough and she was still living at home with her mom. She researched firms and emailed associates who were in the departments she was interested in. She sent over twenty emails and understood that she only needed one yes to initiate a conversation with someone at the company. This strategy proved successful, as she was able to secure three interviews at different companies through her networking efforts. Eventually, she was able to land her first six-figure job at a big firm.

Sample Message to Request Informational Interview

Dear [Name],

I hope this email finds you well. My name is [Your Name], and I'm currently exploring opportunities in [industry/field]. I came across your profile on [LinkedIn/Company website] and was impressed by your experience in [specific area].

I was wondering if you would be open to a 15-20 minute informational interview over the phone or via Zoom. I would love to learn more about your experiences and gain insights into your work in [specific area or industry].

If you're available for an informational interview, please let me know what times work best for you in the next week or two. I'm flexible with my schedule and am happy to work around your availability.

Thank you for your time, and I look forward to hearing from you.

Best regards,

[Your Name]

NEGOTIATING YOUR SALARY FOR A NEW JOB

What if you land the job interview? How do you negotiate pay? Negotiating pay in a job interview can feel awkward if you are not used to advocating for yourself, but it's an important step in securing fair compensation for your work. One effective way to prepare for a pay negotiation is to research the typical salary range for the position you are applying for, both within the company and in the broader industry. This information can help you set realistic expectations and give you the confidence to make a strong case for why you are deserving of a higher salary. Focus on the value you can bring to the company and your unique qualifications, rather than dwelling on your current salary or financial needs. Also, be prepared to show evidence to support your desired salary, whether from industry research or from your previous experience.

Doriane St Fleur, founder of Your Career Girl, a consulting firm specializing in helping her clients, specifically women of color, earn more, gives us this salary negotiation checklist:

CHECKLIST FOR NEGOTIATING SALARY

☑ Have you done your research and you're clear on competitive salary (Glassdoor, LinkedIn, word of mouth)?

☑ Did you wait as long as possible to engage in the salary negotiation conversation (Remember whoever says their number first, loses)?

☑ What is your target salary range (identify your acceptable and aspirational numbers)?

☑ Are there other areas besides salary, you'll need to negotiate (PTO, flex arrangement, etc.)?

☑ What are your non-negotiables?

☑ Are you prepared to explain why you're qualified for your target salary?

☑ Have you thought about your next steps if your terms aren't met (Walk away, ask for first 6 months trial period to revisit salary)?

CREDIT: Doriane St. Fleur, founder of *Your Career Girl*

CREATE INCOME OPPORTUNITIES THROUGH SIDE HUSTLES AND ENTREPRENEURSHIP

Side hustles, gig work, and entrepreneurship can be great ways to earn some extra money quickly. These opportunities range from driving for Uber or Lyft to selling items online.

In this section, we will explore different types of side hustles and gig work that can help you reach your financial goals.

Ask yourself, do you have an interest or talent that you can turn into a side hustle? Is there another stream of income that you can create outside of your normal nine-to-five or regular day job?

Start writing down all of your ideas and then pick a few for further research. You may not be able to implement any of your ideas right away, but it's good to get your creative juices flowing.

Side Hustles

Side hustles refer to the additional income-generating activities pursued alongside your primary source of income. They typically involve utilizing your skills, talents, or resources to undertake part-time or freelance work in order to supplement earnings. Here are some of the more common side hustles your fellow Journeyers have undertaken:

- Develop a freelance business using your skills or talents, such as writing, graphic design, or consulting.

- Offer tutoring or coaching services in a subject you excel at.

- Create a blog or YouTube channel and monetize it through advertising or sponsorships.

- Sell goods online through platforms like Etsy or Amazon.

- Develop a digital product or course and sell it online.

- Rent out a room in your home on Airbnb or similar platforms.

- Offer pet-sitting or dog walking services in your spare time.

- Drive for a ride-sharing service.

- Deliver meals or packages for a food delivery service.

- Rent out your car on Turo or similar platforms.

- Offer handyman services for home repairs or maintenance.

- Clean homes or offices in your spare time.

- Sell unwanted items around your house on websites like eBay or Craigslist.

- Participate in paid online surveys or focus groups.

- Participate in gig economy jobs, such as TaskRabbit or Fiverr.

- Rent out your parking space.

Depending on your level of debt or how far behind you are on your financial goals, you can first think of starting with a low-cost and low-risk side hustle idea that does not require much of an upfront investment—for example, babysitting, dog walking, or tutoring. For quick wins and a way of getting extra cash, you can look at selling unused or lightly used things around your house. An item may be useless to you but valuable to someone else. Go through your closets, garage, cabinets and anywhere else you hide things and see what you can sell online. You can sell on sites like eBay and Craigslist, or find local Facebook groups where people buy and sell things. You can also help family and friends sell their things.

Remember Ariana from earlier, who struggled with budgeting until she found a system that made sense for her? She was working a full-time job and running her side hustle when she realized that her passion for streamlining and organizing could help online business owners. Initially, she made around $100 a month, but her business grew rapidly, and she was soon making thousands of dollars a month. She took a leap of faith and turned her side hustle into a full-time business, making four or five thousand dollars a month.

Entrepreneurship

Entrepreneurship is the process of identifying, creating, and managing a business or venture with the goal of generating profit and creating value. Sometimes your temporary quick side hustle to earn fast cash like selling items or babysitting can turn into a more long-term side hustle or creative endeavor that becomes something you take to the next level and make a full-time business.

Ask yourself, do you have an interest or talent that you can turn into a business? Is there another stream of income that you can create outside of your normal nine-to-five or regular day job?

Start writing down all of your ideas and then pick a few for further research. You may not be able to implement any of your ideas right away, but it's good to get your creative juices flowing. Creating a side hustle or becoming an entrepreneur is a viable way to exponentially increase your income but may take more time and money to start up and sustain.

Tasha was on episode 243 of the podcast. She began her journey in the personal finance space with a blog, documenting her path to debt freedom. One of the ways she was able to earn extra money was through being a Virtual Assistant (VA). Once she realized that her audience was more interested in the "how" part of her debt payoff journey, she pivoted to showing more of her VA gig. From there, Tasha has built an entire VA agency empire, which earns multiple six figures.

Entrepreneurship Tips and Ideas

- Start a business in an industry you're passionate about.

- Develop a product or service that solves a problem or meets a need in the market.

- Develop a mobile app or software program.

- Become a franchise owner of an established business.

- Join a business incubator or accelerator to gain support and resources for your business.

- Crowdfund your business idea through platforms like Kickstarter or Indiegogo.

Creative Outlets and Hobbies

Sometimes what we view as creative work or a hobby that we enjoy can also be a pathway to making money. Of course, you don't have to turn every passion you have into a money-generating idea. Some passions are meant to be explored without being capitalized on. When you put pressure on something you love to make you money, it's possible to lose the joy of it and your creative work sometimes is meant to be an escape from the pressure of thinking about money. But in some cases your hobby or thing you are good at—writing, talking, knitting, painting—can be a pathway to more money.

Journey to Launch, the blog, started out more as a hobby to share my personal journey to FI. I had no intention to make money from it but began to see it as a pathway to contribute to the personal finance conversation online in a meaningful way and get paid for it. This little hobby of mine allowed me to quit my corporate career, start a top-ranked podcast, and write this book you're reading.

IMPROVING MINDSET AND HABITS AROUND INCOME

In order to have the confidence and belief in yourself that you can and do deserve to earn the amount you need to satisfy your financial and life goals, you'll need to understand and reflect on how your current mindset and habits impact your money-making abilities.

If you have been underearning or have not been able to receive what you feel you deserve in pay, it's time to have an honest assessment as to whether limiting beliefs are potentially holding you back, and what they might be. Limiting beliefs are thoughts, either conscious or unconscious, that hold you back from your potential and abilities. These beliefs, which often go unrecognized, can prevent you from wanting to earn more. Examples of limiting beliefs include the idea that in order to make more money, you must compromise your values or change who you are, or that hard, undesirable work is required. Another limiting belief is that earning more money leads to more problems, or that wealthy people are bad or dishonest. Do you look at people who earn a lot and think negatively about them and how they've earned their wealth and status? Deep down do you feel like you don't have the skills or are not smart enough or good enough to earn more?

Let's take a look at how a negative mindset prevents you from earning more money compared to a more positive one. Karla has an entry-level job as an assistant to an executive at a Fortune 500 company. She doesn't have the typical education background to work at the coveted asset manager job that makes twice as much as her and doesn't feel like she could ever get a job like that even though she practically knows as much as anyone else starting out due to her exposure to the decision-makers at the company. She feels stuck in her job and is not happy about her income but doesn't see a pathway to making more.

Compare that to Janine who also starts working as an executive assistant in a similar job and pay scale as Karla. She sees other people hired to sales and management positions and feels that even though she doesn't have the standard educational background as them, she is just as capable of doing the job as them. She begins to volunteer for stretch assignments at work and tells her bosses that she would like to learn more. She even takes advantage of the online classes her company provides, to supplement her learning at the job. When the opportunity comes and there is an open position for the job with the starting salary, who is more likely to get that job? Most likely Janine and unfortunately, Karla, with her way of thinking, may not even consider applying as she can't fathom it would be something attainable for her to have. Janine is operating from the Be-Do-Have model that we talked about earlier in the book. Once you believe you are capable and can grow into the person you need to become, even before the circumstances confirm that you can, nothing will be able to stop you from succeeding.

I can speak to Janine's point of view because in my corporate career, I found myself in similar situations. While working in the administrative side in the real estate investment department, I knew I wanted to work in the Northeast region as an asset manager. It was a higher-paying job with more potential for growth in the company. I did not have the educational background they typically like to hire into the role, but because I worked essentially as an admin with all of the executive leaders in the department, mostly everyone knew who I was. My main task was to schedule deal calls for the executive committee with the other regions. I knew I could do the job of an entry-level asset manager, but there were no openings available.

Since my employer covered the expenses for ongoing education, I decided to go back to school to get my master's degree in real estate from NYU while working in the administrative role. I reasoned that even if the desired job position was not currently available, it was essential to undertake all the necessary preparations in advance, ensuring I was fully equipped for the role if an opportunity came around.

About a year into my program, the coveted asset manager position opened up in the Northeast region. My cubicle was not too far from the head of the Northeast real estate department office, so when I saw the email go out about the position, I sprang into action. I printed out my résumé (which was already updated—stay ready so you don't have to get ready), went to his office, and handed it to him. I told him that I'd be applying formally, but wanted him to know that I'd been waiting for this position to open up. He looked up at me, part impressed and probably part confused, and said, "I just sent this email." I said, "I know, and I wanted to make sure you knew how interested I was." Long story short, I ended up in the role. If I had waited until the position was open before going back to get my master's, or if I didn't have the confidence to express my interest in the role despite not having all the relevant experience, I would not have landed the job.

WHAT'S YOUR INCOME "ENOUGH" POINT?

How much income do you need to earn to give you the desired life you want? How much spending is enough to meet your needs? While I don't think you should put a limit to how much you can earn, you should be aware of how much is enough. Is it possible to earn more than you need? In theory, no, because you can always find uses for more money, whether you keep it and spend it on yourself or donate it to a cause you care about. If the way you make the money is enjoyable or effortless, and the trade-off of time or energy to earn that money is of no consequence to you, by all means earn to the sky's limit. But is there a trade-off that you don't want to sacrifice, like working more, working longer, or doing something you don't want to? There is a price and a threshold where more income is not worthwhile because of what it takes for you to earn it. I've had the opportunity to earn more money in my business but the trade-off of time and energy wasn't worth it to me, so I've either walked away from partnerships or declined opportunities. Walking away from my corporate job was another way in which I chose to leave the security of an income behind in exchange for more time flexibility as a full-time entrepreneur. Working eight hours a day with a three-hour daily commute in exchange for the guaranteed six-figure salary and reaching my financial independence goals earlier was an exchange that I deemed unworthy.

YOUR INCOME, JOURNEYER STAGE, AND GUAC LEVEL

Your Journeyer stage and your desired Guac lifestyle level will determine how focused you are at growing or maintaining an income that supports you. For example, if you are in the early Journeyer stages (Explorer, Cadet, or Aviator) and truly do not earn enough money to accomplish income's four jobs that we talked about earlier (pay for mandatory expenses, reduce liabilities, increase assets, pay for discretionary expenses), then you'll need to put your focus on earning more. If you desire a higher-level Guac lifestyle, then earning enough money to cover your expenses while having enough to invest so that you can maintain that lifestyle in FI is essential.

QUESTIONS TO ASK YOURSELF ABOUT YOUR CURRENT INCOME

- Do you currently earn enough to cover your mandatory expenses, financial goals, and discretionary expenses? And is your income able to fulfill four purposes?

- If yes, are you happy with the pace you're on to reach

your financial independence goals—meaning that if you keep your income and expenses the same without changing anything, are you okay with the time frame it's going to take to reach your goals?

- If yes, keep up what you're doing.

- If no, find ways to increase income.

- If your current income is not able to do its four jobs properly (pay for mandatory expenses, pay down liabilities, increase assets, and pay for discretionary expenses), how much more do you need to earn?

- Are you happy with the way you earn your income?

- Do you want to work less?

- Do you want to change careers?

- Are you living your desired Guac lifestyle level? If not, how much more would you need to earn to live your ideal Guac lifestyle level?

QUESTIONS TO ASK YOURSELF ABOUT SIDE HUSTLES AND ENTREPRENEURSHIP

- Write down three ways in which you can possibly increase your income. Think of a low-start-up side hustle you can do right now to make more money. E.g.: Babysitting, dog walking, house sitting, etc. Just start jotting down everything that comes to mind.

- What are the immediate next two steps you need to do to start each side hustle?

- Are there any specialties or skills that you currently use at your job that can be leveraged to help in a side hustle? E.g., you are a teacher and have a knack for giving instructions to kids. Can you tutor in person or sign up for an online tutoring program as a teacher?

- Are there any interests that you have that can be leveraged into a side hustle? You love working out, gardening, or talking about money so you begin to learn about creating content around foundation topics to share online or in your community.

11

PAY DOWN LIABILITIES

In Chapter 9, we defined what liabilities are and identified them. Now it's time to identify and develop a strategy to repay your debts and decide whether you wish to use debt as a tool on your journey toward financial independence or avoid it altogether.

What you own—your assets—minus what you owe—your liabilities and debts—equals your net worth. Your net worth is an important indicator of where you are on your FI journey because your net worth reflects the value of your assets, which will allow you to become financially independent.

The more you owe, the more you'll have in debt payments, which means the less income you have to spend on mandatory expenses, discretionary expenses, and to grow assets. Starting out in a professional career and dealing with student loans, typically the highest debt for most people, second to their mortgage, can lead to a negative net worth. Add on credit card debt, car loans, and other debts and it's easy to see why so many people are struggling to make headway with their finances.

Many of us encountered debt early in life, when we may not have fully comprehended its long-term repercussions. It could have been through college financial aid offices extending offers to assist us in attending their institution, or credit card companies enticing us on campus with the allure of making purchases without immediate repayment, allowing us to afford more than what we had in cash. You most likely didn't get the guidance or education to understand why you should avoid unnecessary debt and that you shouldn't take on more debt than you needed.

Reducing and eventually eliminating your debt is crucial for achieving FI because it allows you to have fewer obligations to others and gives you the freedom to allocate your income as you see fit. By eliminating debt, you can avoid the burden of making monthly payments to your credit card and carrying a debt balance.

CREATING A PLAN FOR YOUR DEBT

In order to develop an effective debt-payoff plan, you must understand the underlying reasons why you accrued debt in the first place. By taking a few extra minutes now to dig deeper, we can ensure that the results of your efforts will be long-lasting and prevent the recurrence of unnecessary debt in the future.

Just like how stretching before a run can help prevent injuries and make the run less painful, reflecting internally and assessing your behaviors before developing a debt-payoff strategy is like the stretch before the run. It helps you prepare for the actual process of paying off your debt and reduces the likelihood of encountering issues or setbacks.

Go back to the list of debts that you wrote down from Chapter 8. For each debt listed, write what made you accumulate the debt in the first place. The reason for some debts, like student loans, will be more obvious than others. But what about the other debts you've listed? How did they accumulate? What did you spend the money on? Christmas gifts, going out to eat, vacations, an emergency, random shopping? Identify the reason. If you have multiple purchases on a credit card, review your statements and analyze your past spending. Are there any recurring charges or trends, such as frequent restaurant visits, Uber rides, or deliveries?

Questions to ask about the debt:

- Did this purchase bring you joy and/or provide you with convenience?

- Was it worth it?

- If you could go back, would you still make that purchase today knowing what you know now? Why or why not?

Coming to terms with why and how the debt was accumulated in the first place is a good accountability exercise. The answers to these questions will help give you insight to your past behaviors and allow you to be more thoughtful about how you use debt moving forward.

Organize Your Debts

Now we will move into figuring out the actual strategy you want to use in paying off your debt. First we need to organize your debt into one of the three different lists below:

- Lowest to highest outstanding debt balance

- Highest to lowest interest rate debt

- Highest to lowest emotional discomfort/annoyance

(debt that annoys or upsets you the most, regardless of outstanding balance or interest rate)

The three lists are important because they help you to determine your payoff strategy. You can use this guide to rank your debts here.

Determine Your Payoff Strategy

Now that you have your three lists, you can choose the payoff strategy that works best for you. There are two main methods to paying off your debt, the *snowball method* and the *avalanche method*.

The snowball method involves paying off your debts from the smallest to the largest balance, regardless of their interest rates. The advantage of this method is that it allows you to achieve relatively quick wins by eliminating a smaller debt completely, as opposed to starting with a larger balance that would take longer to pay off. This approach can help you build momentum and provide a mental and emotional boost, because you will have one less debt to worry about.

The avalanche method is a debt repayment strategy where you prioritize paying off the debt with the highest interest rate first, followed by the ones with lower interest rates. This method helps you save money on overall interest paid because the higher the interest rate, the more money you are charged on the outstanding balance. By tackling the highest interest rate debt first, you can reduce the amount of interest that accrues over time.

Regardless of the strategy you end up choosing, we will focus on putting any additional cash you have toward paying off one card at a time. You will still pay the minimum payments on all of your credit cards but any extra cash you've allocated for debt payoff will go toward one card until it is paid off. Then, we will focus one by one on the remaining cards until they are all paid off and a distant memory. This will help you focus your efforts and see the best results because your money is going to pay down one card vs. spreading the money around different cards and not being able to see any real progress.

Let's compare these two payoff strategies using the following debt:

Credit Card A Balance: $8,500, 22% interest rate

Credit Card B Balance: $4,000, 8% interest rate

Credit Card C Balance: $1,500, 16% interest rate

Each debt has a minimum payment of $20 per card, and thanks to the work you did to optimize your expenses in Chapter 8 and increase your income in Chapter 9, you've created an extra $300 a month to put toward your debt.

Here's how the pay down looks based on each strategy below:

SNOWBALL METHOD	AVALANCHE METHOD
C: $1,500 - 16% B: $4,000 - 8% A: $8,500 - 22%	A: $8,500 - 22% C: $1,500 - 16% B: $4,000 - 8%

SNOWBALL METHOD:
- Total principal and interest paid: $23,013
- Total Interest paid: $9,024
- Years until debt-free: 5.2 (62 Months)

AVALANCHE METHOD:
- Total principal and interest paid: $19,379
- Total Interest paid: $5,386
- Years until debt-free: 4.3 (52 Months)

Using the avalanche method will save you more money in total interest paid and you'll be credit card debt-free sooner than using the snowball method. However, it will take you longer to pay off that first card using the avalanche method. The snowball method allows you to get rid of the smallest balance card faster but takes you longer to pay off all the debt and you pay more in overall interest.

Also, remember when earlier I asked you to put your debt in the list of most annoying to least annoying regardless of interest rate or balance? You can also use that as a factor in the order you want to pay off your debt. Let's say you had one credit card balance due to a purchase that you regret and want to get rid of because it brings up uneasy feelings—you can start with that debt first.

Determining your motivation is crucial. If your primary motivation is to save tangible money, then the avalanche method may work better for you. If you are driven by achieving quicker wins and reducing the number of cards you have, then the snowball method may be a better fit. However, if your motivation stems from emotional reasons and you want to eliminate the debt that bothers you the most, then prioritize paying off the debt that causes you the most stress, regardless of logic or math. Remember that you have the freedom to customize your path and strategy based on what works for you.

More Debt Payoff Strategy Tips

- If you can pay off a single debt regardless of the interest rate within six months or less and that will give you a morale boost, focus on that and then focus on one of the other strategies. It's a quick easy win.

- If your debt interest rates are similar, e.g. 20%, 21%, 22%, then it doesn't make sense to split hairs as the difference in paying one down according to interest rates is negligible since they are so close together. Use the snowball method.

- If the balances are similar, then pick the avalanche method.

- If a particular debt causes you more angst and emotional burden than another, make that debt payoff a priority, regardless of the interest rate or loan balance. Knocking out the loans that alleviate negative feelings will improve your morale.

- It's up to you to pick the strategy that works for your circumstances. I encourage you to pick one and stick with it. Just like advancing through different Journeyer levels, paying off debt and staying motivated is a marathon and not a sprint, and you must persevere. If it took you several years to accumulate your debt, don't anticipate that you can pay it all back in just a few months. Monitor your progress, track how your balance decreases every three months, and celebrate every small milestone you achieve. Your feelings about your finances and the progress you make toward your objectives are crucial. Ultimately, whichever method keeps you motivated is the right one for you.

COMMIT TO THE DEBT PAYOFF JOURNEY

If you are in the Explorer or Cadet phase, pledge to yourself that you will not use credit cards or take on any further debt going forward unless it is a legitimate emergency or falls under the necessary category to live or be safe, e.g., your furnace breaks in the middle of winter or you need new tires. If it's a discretionary item and it can't be paid for in full at the time of purchase, you can't afford it at the moment.

IMPROVING MINDSET AND HABITS: LETTING GO OF SHAME AND LIMITING BELIEFS

Working on releasing the shame we feel around debt is crucial because that shame causes us to shut down or avoid confronting how we can fix it. According to recent data from the Federal Reserve, as of 2021, approximately 80% of American households have some form of debt. This includes mortgages, student loans, credit card debt, and other forms of consumer debt.

This idea of not worrying about it and dealing with it later doesn't make the problem go away but only makes it bigger. The same way compounding interest works in your favor when it comes to growing your money with your investments, it works against you when growing your debt. If you only pay the minimum on your debt, the outstanding balance of what you owe grows bigger. It's the reason why you can graduate with $40,000 in student loan debt and then in ten years owe $120,000. Or why your credit card balance only continues to increase even though you may be paying slightly over the minimum. Unfortunately, debt is a common and widespread issue affecting millions of people across different age groups and income levels, but just because it's a common problem does not mean it has to be your problem to deal with forever. This is why implementing the strategies in this chapter and doing the mindset work that we are going to talk about in the next couple sections is key.

LIES AND LIMITING BELIEFS KEEPING YOU IN DEBT CYCLE

As you work to begin paying down your debt, I want to address some limiting beliefs and lies that you may have told yourself in the past so that you can identify when they are coming up again as you move forward with paying off debt.

Lie #1: You Need Luxury to Feel Good about Yourself or Validated

Advertisers have done a great job in making you feel like you deserve their products. Do you think it's by accident that after you see a BMW commercial or Chanel advertisement you feel a sense of longing and yearning, telling yourself that you deserve to have those products? Companies spend millions of dollars figuring out the best way to market to you and how to make you feel like you can't live without their products.

Ask yourself these two questions when looking at a luxury purchase: Why do you like that product? Do you like the actual quality of the product or the status symbol that owning that product brings you? Whatever your answer is won't be wrong, but if you're not in a position to truly afford the luxury you want, then you are making your current financial situation harder.

Lie #2: You Can Afford It

Just because you have the money in your bank account, doesn't mean you can really afford a purchase. Every dollar should already be earmarked for something and have a job—hello, budget. Even if you convince yourself that you can indulge in a new pair of shoes or a fancy dinner since you have funds in your account, in reality that money would be better spent paying off a bill or reducing your debt. This is why having a budget is key so that you can make these buying decisions from an informed place.

Lie #3: It's Not That Much Money

Using your credit card to gradually spend money on smaller, low-cost items like buying lunch on a daily basis can accumulate over time, leading to a significant expense. When reviewing your expenses, particularly your credit card statements, assess the amount of money spent on these small purchases that eventually contribute to the larger sum you now have to pay off.

Lie #4: You Only Live Once (YOLO)

YOLO only works if your life is unexpectedly cut short, because otherwise you still wake up the next day and have more debt than you did the day before. While it's true that life is fleeting, it's important to consider the future and not spend money you don't have recklessly.

Lie #5: You'll Never Get Out of Debt Anyway

This is one of the most dangerous debt-limiting beliefs of all because it keeps you in a perpetual cycle of debt. If you have a lot of debt, you may choose to just continue spending and piling on more debt since you feel your situation is too far gone to correct. This negative thinking will keep you forever stuck and put you on a never-ending debt accumulation cycle. You have to believe that you can do it. The changes won't happen overnight and you have to celebrate your small wins so that you feel encouraged to continue on.

FREQUENTLY ASKED QUESTIONS AND COMMON SCENARIOS AROUND DEBT

In this section, I will be addressing some frequently asked questions and common scenarios such as whether you should consolidate debt or do 0% transfers, whether it's a good idea to never use debt again, and whether you should invest while in debt. Let's take a look at each of these topics.

Should You Consolidate Debt or Do 0% Balance Transfers?

You may have received offers in the mail or online inviting you to open a new credit card and transfer your outstanding credit card balances to the new card at a 0% introductory rate for one year, or to take out a new loan at a lower interest rate and use that money to pay off the higher interest rate debt. Mathematically, it's tempting to do this and can work, but you need to be careful. This is a good strategy to use if you can commit and stick with not using your credit cards again and paying off the credit card before the interest rate kicks in. If you haven't addressed the issue that got you into debt, you are most likely just kicking the can farther down the road and may end up with a bigger balance at the end of it all. You'll need to employ the mindset and behavior adjustments when it comes to your debt in order to not repeat the same mistakes. It's why actually completing the debt assessment is so important as a way to uncover the root of what got you into debt in the first place.

Once I Get Out of Debt, Should I Avoid It Completely?

You can decide how you want your relationship to debt to be going forward. It's completely okay if you want to avoid credit cards and other debts moving forward on your journey. Your relationship with debt could have been so traumatizing, whether it was the length of time it took you to get out of it, thinking back to the mistakes you made getting into debt, or just simply not wanting to ever feel like you owe anyone or anything something again. If you are one of those people, I am not going to try and change your mind about pursuing and living a debt-free life.

But if you feel like you are in the right emotional place and are self-disciplined enough to manage access to debt and use it in a way where you are in control and to your benefit, keep reading, I'll talk more about using debt as a tool later in this chapter.

Should I Invest while in Debt?

The question of "Should I invest while still in debt?" comes up more times that I can count from people who want to invest but are still in debt. There are some experts who take the stance that you shouldn't invest while in debt and that all debt is bad. While paying off your consumer debt should be a top priority, it shouldn't be your only priority. You can't afford to wait until you are out of debt to invest, especially if the time frame to become debt-free is longer than one year. For marginalized people and people of color already severely behind on their retirement and net worth and who also have a proportionally higher balance of debt including student loan debt, telling us to wait to invest further hinders our ability to catch up to our white counterparts.

Your ability to invest while in debt will look different depending on the Journeyer stage you are in. The only stage where I will tell you to hold off on starting to invest (and that's only if you haven't already started because I wouldn't tell you to stop investing in your 401(k) if you have already started) is in the Explorer stage. The reason for this is because Explorer is meant to be a temporary short-term stage. This is the stage where you are not able to cover your current expenses with your current income. At this stage you'll need to focus your effort on getting stable. My goal and hope for anyone in this stage is that you are not here for longer than one to three months because in this stage the goal is to simply be able to have your income cover your mandatory expenses without having to go into additional debt. In this stage I recommend not focusing on investing because if you follow the steps and advice in the previous chapters, you won't be in that stage for long. Investing is all about leapfrogging your wealth because your investments get to grow exponentially instead of in a linear way.

After reaching stability and entering into the Cadet stage where you are focused on paying off debt, investing should also be added to your priority list. In the Cadet stage, you don't need to necessarily max out your retirement account, but you should contribute something to it, even if it is the minimum to get a company match or it's what you deem a small or insignificant amount. Even investing $50 a month in your Roth IRA or 401(k) for the next twenty years at an average 8% return will grow to $29,000 (compared to only saving $50 a month for the next twenty years in a savings account that earns 0.05% which will get you to $12,000). Investing something right now, even if you are in debt and even if it's not the amount you'd like it to be, is moving the needle on your wealth and forces you to flex your investing muscle. I guarantee that over time and quicker than you think, you will gain the necessary skills to increase your cash flow and be able to invest more. That $50 a month now may only be for a year or two while you work to get out of debt and then you'll be able to double or triple it. People assume their investment contributions will always be the same amount or linear and that's not the case. In different stages of your life and under different circumstances, the amounts you'll be able to contribute will change. So instead of $50 a month for twenty years, it's $50 a month for one year, then $200 a month for years two to five, and then $600 a month after. Waiting until you have it all figured out or until you're completely debt-free means you'll be waiting indefinitely and on the off chance you do decide to begin at some distant point in the future, you would have already missed out on so much valuable time. I'm not asking you to look back and regret what you haven't done yet or the time you've missed to take action; that's in the past and blaming yourself for inaction when you can't change history only will keep you stuck. As the Chinese proverb says, "The best time to plant a tree was twenty years ago. The second best time is now."

Can Debt Be Used for Good?

I don't think all debt is bad and sometimes debt is necessary. There I said it. While I'm a big proponent of paying off and eliminating consumer debt as fast as possible, I'm also an advocate of using debt responsibly as part of our financial and life toolbox. Without discipline and a clear plan, debt is dangerous. With self-control and strategy, debt can be used in a responsible way to help us reach our financial and life goals. The following examples are situations where using debt is practical and helps us reach our goals.

→ BUYING A HOME

Some of our most important purchases and investments would not be possible without having access to debt. For a vast majority of people, including myself, purchasing a home would not be possible without having a mortgage. Although some people argue that owning a home is not an investment due to not being able to quickly access the equity you build in the home, and the potential costs of ownership compared to renting, the average person's wealth is largely derived from the equity in their home. For many, home ownership is a key way to build wealth in the present—and for future generations. When using a mortgage to buy a home, you should buy something affordable and within your means so that you are not stuck with mortgage payments or property taxes that you can't manage. When purchasing your primary residence, treat it as an investment and conduct a thorough evaluation to ensure that you can truly afford the purchase. This involves taking into account factors such as the current mortgage interest rates in the market, the area in which you are purchasing and its current prices, and the rental prices in case you wish to move and rent it out.

→ PAYING FOR COLLEGE

Many professions still require a college education and degree, which can often involve taking out student loans even if you attend a less expensive school like a community college. It's crucial to borrow only what you need to complete your education, whether it covers tuition, room and board, or living expenses. You should carefully consider your chosen degree and future earning potential when looking at the loans required for your education. If you plan to switch careers or pursue advanced degrees that can boost your earning potential, it may be worth taking out a loan, but you'll need to weigh the pros and cons. Research the income potential for that career with that degree or certification to determine whether the higher income will offset the cost of obtaining the degree.

→ EARNING FREE TRAVEL AND OTHER PERKS

Using your credit card to earn points for cash back allows you to save money on things you would typically spend money on anyway, like groceries and everyday necessities. You can even use your points to pay for things like vacations or splurge items. If you are charging items on your credit card to earn points, you'll need to pay off your balance in full every month so that you don't pay additional interests and fees. For many, using a credit card on a day-to-day basis is not ideal, but for those that have their finances in order, it can be a good way to save or earn money. Many of my flights are paid for by my credit card travel rewards points.

→ HAVING ACCESS TO MONEY IN CASE OF AN EMERGENCY

Sometimes big emergencies will happen, such as car repair or a broken furnace in the middle of winter and you don't yet have the funds saved up to pay for it. In situations like this, having access to a credit card or a home equity line is crucial. This is a much better alternative than having to resort to predatory lenders or so-called payday loans, which are short-term and high-cost loans ranging from $100 to $1,000, and typically have annual interest rates of 400% or more. The finance charge for borrowing $100 ranges from $15 to $30, and for two-week loans, the interest rates can range from 390% to 780% APR. In comparison, credit cards have an average interest rate of only 15%–30%.

Debt in the Later Journeyer Stages

If you are in the later stages of your financial journey in the Aviator, Commander, or Captain stage, then you've intentionally already got out of your consumer debt but still may have mortgage or student loan debt. I often talk about the acceptance of your mortgage debt and student loan debt as debt you live with and manage. It doesn't mean you shouldn't aim to pay them off early. If you've determined that being completely debt-free, student loans and mortgage included, is what will make you feel financially secure then you should focus on that next in addition to continuing to invest. On the other hand, if you've determined that the interest rate on your mortgage or student loan debt is manageable enough to pay them incrementally while still keeping some money for investing or increasing your quality of life (as opposed to paying off all of your debts at once) then do that instead. There isn't necessarily a blanket right or wrong way to do this since it really depends on what you want out of your life. This is the point where you possess the ability to make conscious decisions from a position of empowerment regarding your debt. You have the freedom to choose what actions you want to take, not solely based on prioritizing financial optimization but instead prioritizing what feels right for you, numbers be damned. You can have that kind of flexibility once you've gotten to the Aviator stage and beyond and as long as you understand that there are trade-offs of spending more in the short term and not optimizing for numbers but for immediate happiness could mean a longer timeline to reach complete financial independence.

	DEBT PAYOFF STRATEGY	INVEST WHILE IN DEBT?
EXPLORER	Paying minimum while getting on track and financially stable to cover household expenses.	Not unless you are already investing because your focus here is to be able to cover your expenses. This stage is about survival and we don't want you to be in it long.
CADET	Aggressively paying off high-interest rate debt like credit cards, personal loans, and other loans such as car loans.	Yes, up until company match if available. Can split any additional extra cash between investing and paying off debt.

12

INCREASE ASSETS

Increasing your assets is critical to being able to reach FI. Your assets give you the money to support your lifestyle and expenses. Without assets that provide you passive income, you'll have no choice but to actively work for money. In this chapter we'll talk about saving money and investing money.

Saving refers to setting aside money on a regular basis, typically in a low-risk account such as a savings account, money market account, or high-yield savings account. Because there is minimum to no risk, the return on these accounts is lower.

Investing, on the other hand, involves putting money into various types of assets, such as stocks, bonds, and real estate, with the expectation of earning a higher return over time. I'll often see people mistakenly use the terms "saving" and "investing" interchangeably when discussing their long-term goals, particularly regarding retirement. I believe it is essential to differentiate between the two since people may assume that saving alone is enough to reach their objectives. While traditional saving is necessary, it will not be enough if you aspire to achieve FI.

MY SAVING AND INVESTING STORY

By saving money, I gained the ability to seize opportunities that would have been inaccessible to me without financial stability. However, it was through investing that I was able to accelerate my journey toward FI and wealth accumulation.

Although my mother never explicitly taught me financial lessons, she did emphasize the significance of saving money. At the age of around six, my mother took me to open my first bank account and stressed the importance of saving a portion of every dollar earned. Regardless of how small the amount, even if it was just five cents, my mother believed in saving for the possibility of an unforeseen opportunity to advance in life. When you don't have a lot, saving and making a dollar stretch is necessary to survive and get ahead. If you have a drive and vision for a better life, having limited income forces you to become adept at maximizing your available resources. I find this particularly true when it comes to many immigrants who come to the United States wanting a better life and more opportunities. My mother arrived in the United States at twenty years old with no money and nothing to her name. She had to leave me behind in Jamaica with my grandmother while she navigated and figured out the system on her own. My mom relied on her father's family for a place to initially stay for the first couple of weeks and then moved in with a cousin who was a manager of Kentucky Fried Chicken and got her a job working there.

Since I was still back in Jamaica, she budgeted her small earnings and sent back money out of each paycheck to my grandmother to take care of me.

After my grandmother and I arrived in New York a year later to join my mother, we all moved in together with another family member. My mother pursued her college education and had to rely on government assistance to cover my daycare expenses and our basic needs while she went to school full-time. Through my mother's resourcefulness and determination she was able to earn her associate's then moved on to get her bachelor's degree. After securing her first entry-level position and after saving up some money, we were able to move into our own apartment. Additionally, I witnessed my grandmother skillfully managing her earnings as a nanny to support her expenses and eventually purchase a house with a combination of a small settlement and her savings.

I saw firsthand how earning, saving, and managing money could lead to significant improvements in our lives, culminating in the achievement of my grandmother owning her own home and my mom getting her master's degree and eventually working her way into a solid career with great income. It's no wonder why saving money became one of my superpowers. But in order to have and save money, you need a job. I've had a job since the age of fourteen through the NYC summer youth program where I scrubbed cafeteria tables for summer school students. The next summer, I worked off the books at a small lawyer's office in the city doing office work. During my teenage years, I also worked at the Brooklyn Public Library and Bed Bath & Beyond, and made a conscious effort to save some of my earnings no matter how much I made.

In college, I applied for the InRoads internship program, which provided minority students with an opportunity to work for Fortune 500 companies at a competitive salary. After being accepted into the program during my freshman year, I had to interview with multiple companies to find a good match. Although I interviewed with three companies, I wasn't selected by any of them and the program was fast approaching. In the final hour, I interviewed with MetLife, one of the largest insurance companies in the US, and they selected me, or perhaps they had no other option as the deadline was quickly approaching. I vividly recall receiving my first paycheck, which was over $1,000, as this was the most money I had ever received in one check until that point. Even my previous jobs on campus and in high school only paid me a few hundred dollars. My first instinct, despite the larger paycheck, was to pretend like I was still only receiving a couple hundred dollars and to save 80% of the check. I stayed with MetLife as an InRoads intern throughout college and worked every summer and even went back to work on my winter break one year.

With my college campus job during the school year and my InRoads intern paycheck, saving between 50%–80% of my paychecks put me in a solid place as a college student; it's why I was somewhat prepared to take advantage of the opportunity to buy real estate upon graduating college at twenty years old in Dumbo, Brooklyn. Saving is also how my mom had enough money to help me with the initial 10% down payment needed to go into contract on the property. She at that point did not own anything for herself but dug into and drained her savings to help me with a portion of the down payment. It would take two more years after signing the initial contract and a lot more saving to come up with the additional 10% and closing costs to close on the condo.

During my high school and college years, I wasn't entirely sure what I was saving for. You just never know when you will have the opportunity of a lifetime to advance yourself or get to the next rung of life's ladder with the help of that money. Saving money not only gives you a cushion and peace of mind if something goes wrong but it provides a springboard for you to reach higher for something. With the money I had saved, I was able to buy my first home that turned into my most profitable investment, my condo in Dumbo. Years later after discovering FI, I was able to switch from an aggressive saving mindset to an investing mindset where I invested a majority of my money after paying for expenses into my retirement and non-retirement accounts. The difference in switching to just a saving mindset to an investment mindset catapulted me on this journey.

The chart below breaks down what you save for and the types of accounts you use for savings goals, and what you invest for vs. the types of accounts you use for investing goals.

SAVING

SAVING FOR:	SAVING IN (Types of Saving Accounts):
• Emergency Fund • Quality of Life Events & Lifestyle Goals (House Down Payment, Car, Vacations) • FU Fund	• Traditional Savings Account • Online High-Yield Savings Account • Money Market Account

INVESTING

INVESTING FOR:	INVESTING IN (Types of Investment Accounts):
• Traditional Retirement • Financial Independence & Early Retirement • Children's College	• Tax Advantaged Retirement Investment Accounts (401(k), 403(b), 457, Trad IRA, Roth IRA, etc.) • Taxable Accounts • 529 Account

Traditional Savings Accounts: Basic type of bank account that offers low interest rates compared to other savings options. Typically provides easy access to funds and is found at traditional brick-and-mortar banks.

Money Market Accounts: A type of savings account that offers higher interest rates than a traditional savings account. May have requirements on a minimum balance or restrictions on withdrawals depending on the institution.

High-Yield Savings Accounts: Similar to a traditional savings account but with higher interest rates and offers competitive rates compared to standard savings accounts. Typically can be found at digital online banks and institutions.

PRIORITIZING YOUR SAVING GOALS

There are so many things you either need to save for out of necessity (emergencies) and proactive financial planning (upcoming events or big purchases). The emergency savings and three- to six-month fund protects you in case something happens to your income. Then there are things you want to save for because they are a goal or desire for you to accomplish or have like buying a home or travel. Your life goals and savings objectives can take precedence over financial goals, and can be pursued at any stage of the Journeyer process. For instance, if you are in debt but expecting a baby and have limited resources, you may need to prioritize saving for baby-related expenses rather than allocating extra cash to debt repayment. It's unrealistic to expect that you won't want to buy a home or have a baby until you're completely out of consumer debt.

It is common to feel overwhelmed by the challenge of achieving all of your savings goals. Therefore, it is necessary to concentrate and devise a plan on which goals to prioritize first, taking into account your Journeyer stage.

For example:

- $1,000–$5,000 emergency fund (Cadet Journeyer stage).

- Three- to six-month full emergency fund (Cadet and Aviator Journeyer stages).

- Saving for life events and quality of life goals (any Journeyer stage).

- Six to twelve months of FU fund for gaps in income or big life changes (Aviator Journeyer stage).

- Saving for having a baby (any Journeyer stage).

- Saving for house down payment and closing costs (Cadet, Aviator, Commander, or Captain Journeyer stage).

$1,000–$5,000 Small Emergency Fund

The amount of this fund typically ranges from $1,000 to $5,000. Although $1,000 may seem like a small amount, it serves as a good starting point if you do not have any savings set aside for emergencies. If you don't have one already, you should open up a separate savings account from your checking account where you can keep this money. This amount also acts like a jump start to your three- to six-month full emergency fund. The objective is to accumulate sufficient funds to handle unexpected expenses, such as replacing a tire or paying a smaller medical bill. It is essential to be prepared for such situations so that they do not derail your financial progress. A small emergency fund instills confidence, knowing that you have a fallback reserve in case of a crisis. In the early Journeyer stages, having an emergency fund is crucial because the margin for cash flow errors is narrower. It is vital to establish a small emergency fund to cover unforeseen expenses that require immediate cash. Missing an important payment or having to rely on credit cards can quickly lead to reverting to old habits and feeling demotivated, particularly when you are just starting out.

Three- to Six-Month Full Emergency Fund

Once you have a small emergency fund saved up, you can begin working on an emergency fund that can cover your basic needs and expenses should you experience a loss in income or there is a bigger emergency that comes up. The typical advice is to save three to six months' worth of expenses. You will be working on saving up this amount in tandem with paying off your debt so this is typically a goal you'll be working on throughout your Cadet and Aviator stages.

Once you've calculated your budget and have an understanding of what your expenses are (from Chapter 9), the mandatory must-haves and the discretionary nice-to-haves, you can begin to determine what a three- to six-month emergency fund looks like. For a bare-bones just what you need, you can look at only your mandatory expenses. If your income were to be disrupted for three to six months, what would you absolutely need to pay in order to stay in your home, pay the bills, and feed yourself and family? If you want to also throw in the nice-to-have, discretionary components of your expenses, you can do that too, just note that the amount you'll need to save will be more.

For example, let's say it costs you $5,000 a month to live according to your bare-bones expenses which include mortgage/rent, groceries, bills, minimum credit card payments, etc., then you'd need $15,000 for a three-month emergency fund to $30,000 for a six-month emergency fund. Remember, that doesn't include any of your nice-to-haves like gym membership, restaurants, or beauty appointments. If you wish to account for these expenses to be realistic about your spending during an emergency, you should calculate your full three- to six-month budget amount. For instance, if your total monthly budget is $7,000, your three-month emergency fund should be $21,000, and your six-month emergency fund should be $42,000.

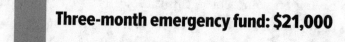

Monthly budget: $7,000

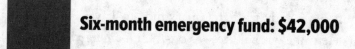

Three-month emergency fund: $21,000

Six-month emergency fund: $42,000

When this number is calculated it can feel defeating and overwhelming because of how much it can be. The important thing to remember here is that this amount is not something you need to save by tomorrow or in the next few months. This can very well take a few years to properly fund. Also, emergencies will likely happen while you are working to save up and you will need to dip into the fund which may make you feel like you are taking steps backward and trying to fill up a bucket with a leak in it. But it's not a sign of defeat and you shouldn't feel like your progress is in vain. This is the entire point of the emergency fund, to be able to use it when you need it.

You can also look at it in a way that allows for flexibility in how you view your emergency fund. If you have $25,000 saved, you can either look at it as five months' worth of bare-bones expenses or three months of full-blown expenses. The important thing is to build a financially fluid and flexible life so that you can change your expenses as needed. You want to be able to adapt your lifestyle and behaviors according to what you need in that moment or in the case of looking at your financial journey, the season of life that you are in or your Journeyer stage.

Saving for Life Events and Quality of Life

When it comes to saving specifically for life events in the near or far-out future, you'll need to be proactive. There are some life events that we can't predict or know that we need to save for yet—that's the beauty and unpredictability of life.

Life's unpredictability adds to its charm, and though there may be unforeseeable events that we cannot prepare for, there are certain goals we set for ourselves that we can plan for. We will look back at some of the goals you've set for yourself and see how we can begin to prepare for them now.

Saving for Life Events and Quality of Life (Order Will Depend on Your Goals)

- Six to twelve months of FU fund for gaps in income or big life changes

- Saving for having a baby

- Saving for house down payment and closing costs

- Saving for travel

- Saving for other big purchases

Saving for bigger purchases or in advance for lifestyle upgrades or improvements to your quality of life can also begin to be factored into your savings plan once you have your baseline $1,000 emergency savings fund established. As you continue to contribute to building up your bigger three- to six-month emergency savings, think ahead to the things you want to be able to do. You can refer back to the goals you established in Chapter 6 and 7 and the priorities you've assigned them. You can save for your three- to six-month emergency savings fund and your life goals at the same time. Remember that saving up a fully funded emergency fund can take years so you shouldn't stop thinking about or working toward your life goals just because you are in the earlier Journeyer stages. Over that time, you will be experiencing your life and will want to live it in a way that feels fulfilled. To ignore saving toward your life goals would be to ignore what gives you fulfillment and would lead to a dull life and journey. Once you get out of the Explorer stage (remember your goal is to get out of this stage as quickly as possible), you can determine the intensity and length of time you want to stay in each following stage based on the lifestyle you want to lead today while understanding the trade-offs of how long it will take you to get to FI.

MULTIPLYING YOUR ASSETS THROUGH INVESTING

Investing can help you build your assets in several ways. For some, real estate investments serve as a significant or primary source of income, while others rely solely on investment accounts for income from their investment portfolio. Some people use a combination of both methods. There is no right or wrong way to invest, as it depends on your risk tolerance, access to investment capital, and desired level of involvement in managing your investments. In this context, I will primarily discuss a boring but effective investment approach through tax-advantaged and taxable accounts using index funds. Before diving into that, let's explore why investing is crucial and why achieving FI is impossible without it.

Just saving money in a savings account is like running on a treadmill that keeps you in place—your money loses value over time in a savings account because of inflation, as well as the increase in the general price of goods and services over time. The average return on a traditional savings account can be as low as 0.05% or up to 0.25%. This means that over twenty years, at the more generous 0.25% rate, your $10,000 would grow to $10,512. Although you don't lose any money, inflation will have diminished your buying power: the cost of something priced $2.50 today will cost you $4.50 in twenty years. I remember growing up going to my favorite pizza shop, a slice of pizza was $1.25. Now, twenty-plus years later, the same slice of pizza from the same pizza shop is $3.25. That's how inflation works in real life. So while saving money will help, it won't provide you with the fuel you'll need to reach financial independence much less sustain the quality of life you deem comfortable in the future. You have to invest, whether you want to reach complete financial independence or not in order to build true wealth. Remember that example above where I talked about your money growing to only $10,512 amount in a savings account. If you were to invest that same starting balance of $10,000 into index funds and not contribute anything else to it and let it sit and grow over a twenty-year period at an average 8% return you'd have $46,610 instead.

This is the power of investing. You can use time and compound interest to your advantage, to help your money grow at a more accelerated rate than it would if it were sitting in a savings account or under your mattress. That's not to say that you shouldn't have money for emergencies in a regular savings account. You should, but you also should be investing your money if you want to build wealth and reach your financial independence goals.

Another way to think of this concept is that saving is like adding and investing is like multiplying:

SAVING		INVESTING
$2 + 6 = 8$	vs.	$2 \times 6 = 12$
$2 + 2 + 4 = 8$	vs.	$2 \times 2 \times 4 = 16$

INVESTMENT ACCOUNT VS. INVESTMENTS

An investment account is what is used to hold your investments. When you buy something like an investment it needs to be held in an investment account. The investments are what you buy such as individual stocks, bonds, index funds, mutual funds, REITs, etc. (which we will define shortly).

There is often confusion between the concepts of investments and investment accounts, as people tend to use these terms interchangeably. However, they are fundamentally different even though they can be related. This can create confusion when starting to invest. Just having an investment account doesn't necessarily mean that you have investments. For instance, when you open a Roth IRA, which is an investment account, with a company like Vanguard or Fidelity, both financial services companies that primarily offer investment management services, you'll need to fund the account by connecting your bank account or transferring money. The money is usually placed in a money market account, which is the equivalent of cash and doesn't generate income. In this scenario, you have an investment account but no income-producing investments. To move forward, you need to purchase the investments you want with the money you have deposited. I've seen many people make the mistake of opening up their investment account which is a huge first step but then forgetting to go back and buy their investments.

Retirement accounts are investment accounts like 401(k)s, 403(b)s, 457s, Traditional IRAs, and Roth IRAs. They are accounts that give you a tax advantage, meaning there is some type of tax incentive or advantage to you contributing to them. Pre-tax retirement accounts like 401(k)s and Traditional IRAs are accounts where you don't pay taxes on the money that you put into them, but you pay taxes on the amount you contributed plus the growth when you withdraw it in retirement.

With post-tax retirement accounts like Roth 401(k)s and Roth IRAs, you already paid taxes on that money that goes into the account and don't pay any taxes on your contribution or growth when you withdraw money from that account.

Sometimes an employer will do what's called a "401(k) match" which is where they also put money in your 401(k) to match your contribution up to a certain amount, which makes contributing to a 401(k) even more advantageous. You can look at this as free money or money that you didn't have to contribute but get to keep as long as you're vested, even if you leave the company. Vesting at a company refers to the process of earning ownership or entitlement to benefits over time or based on certain conditions. Make sure you understand your company's vesting policy. Any money you put in your 401(k) is yours no matter if you decide to leave or stay with the company; you can take it with you when you leave as long as that money is vested. The company may require that you stay with them for a minimum amount of time before the money they contribute to the 401(k) is officially yours to keep when you leave.

Taxable investing accounts are investments that you can open on your own not associated with an employer and that have no tax advantages. You have already paid taxes on the money you put in and will pay taxes on the amount of money made, gains, dividends, and interest.

Investing is the act of expending money into something with the intention of getting more out of it than you put into it.

An **investment** is the asset or thing you acquire or have ownership in.

The **investor** is the person who owns the assets and invests.

TYPES OF INVESTMENT ACCOUNTS

Tax-advantaged retirement investment accounts come in two types: pre-tax and post-tax accounts. The distinction lies in how taxes are handled. On the other hand, there are non-tax-advantaged accounts called taxable accounts, which lack any tax benefits and are not intended for retirement savings. I'll break down the differences between all the accounts below before moving on to the investments you can buy in each account.

Tax-Advantaged Retirement Accounts (Pre-Tax Accounts and Post-Tax Accounts)

Pre-Tax Retirement Accounts: Retirement accounts where contributions are made on a pre-tax basis meaning that they reduce your taxable income in the year in which they are made and are deducted from your paycheck before taxes are taken out. The contributions and any earnings grow tax-deferred until the money is withdrawn during retirement. At that point, taxes are due on the money withdrawn at the individual's ordinary income tax rate. There are limits on how much can be contributed each year, and there may be penalties for withdrawing money before age fifty-nine and a half.

Below are some examples of pre-tax retirement accounts:

- 401(k): An employer-sponsored retirement plan. Employers may offer matching contributions (employer company match %) up to a certain percentage of the employee's contribution, which can help boost retirement savings.

- 403(b): A retirement plan similar to a 401(k) but offered by certain tax-exempt organizations, such as schools and nonprofit organizations.

- 457 Plan: A tax-advantaged retirement plan offered to

employees of state and local governments and some nongovernmental organizations. Unlike the 401(k) and 403(b) plans, contributions to a 457 plan are not subject to the early withdrawal penalty if withdrawn after separation from service, but are still subject to ordinary income tax.

- Traditional IRA: A personal retirement account that an individual can set up at a financial institution, such as a bank or brokerage firm that allows you to make tax-deductible contributions to your retirement savings. There are contribution limits to how much you can contribute.

- Solo 401(k): This is a type of 401(k) plan that is designed for self-employed individuals with no employees. It allows you to make contributions as both an employer and an employee.

Post-Tax Retirement Accounts: Retirement accounts that allow you to make contributions with after-tax dollars. This means that you've already paid taxes on the money you're contributing, so the contributions do not reduce your taxable income in the year you contribute. However, the earnings on your contributions grow tax-free, and qualified withdrawals (after age fifty-nine and a half and a minimum of five years since opening the account) are also tax-free.

Below are examples of post-tax retirement accounts:

- Roth IRA: A personal retirement account that an individual can set up at a financial institution, such as a bank or brokerage firm, that allows you to make after-tax contributions. There are limits to how much you can contribute and there are income limits for contributing to a Roth IRA, and if your income exceeds these limits, your contribution limit may be reduced or eliminated altogether. Generally, contributions can be withdrawn at any time, tax-free and penalty-free. However, earnings on those contributions must meet certain requirements to be withdrawn tax-free and penalty-free.

• Roth 401(k): Employer-sponsored retirement plan that combines features of a traditional 401(k) and a Roth IRA. With a Roth 401(k), employees can choose to contribute a portion of their income on an after-tax basis, which means the money is taxed before it is deposited into the account.

Non-Tax-Advantaged Investment Accounts (Taxable Accounts)

Taxable Accounts: Taxable accounts, also known as regular brokerage accounts or non-retirement accounts, do not offer any tax advantages. With these accounts, you contribute money that has already been taxed, and any investment gains are also subject to taxation. When you withdraw money from a taxable retirement account, you will need to pay taxes on any capital gains, dividends, or interest earned.

Now let's talk about the investment assets that can be bought and held in both your tax-advantaged retirement investment accounts (pre-tax accounts and post-tax accounts) and your non-tax-advantaged investment accounts (taxable accounts).

Types of investment assets:

- Individual Stocks: A stock is a type of security that represents ownership in a company. An individual stock refers to a single share of ownership in a specific company that is publicly traded on a stock exchange.

- Bonds: A bond is a type of debt security in which an investor lends money to an issuer, typically a corporation or government entity, in exchange for regular interest payments and the return of the principal investment at maturity.

- Mutual Funds: A mutual fund is a type of investment vehicle that pools money from multiple investors to purchase a diversified portfolio of stocks, bonds, or other securities. Investors in the mutual fund own a proportionate share of the fund's assets and receive a portion of the fund's gains or losses.

- Index Funds: An index fund is a type of mutual fund or exchange-traded fund (ETF) that tracks a specific market index, such as the S&P 500. Rather than attempting to beat the market, index funds aim to match the performance of the index they track.

- Target Date Funds: A target date fund is a type of mutual fund or ETF that adjusts its asset allocation over time based on a specific target retirement date. As the target date approaches, the fund shifts its portfolio to become more conservative, with a greater allocation to fixed-income securities.

- ETFs: An exchange-traded fund (ETF) is a type of investment fund that trades on a stock exchange, like a stock. ETFs can hold a variety of assets, including stocks, bonds, and commodities, and offer investors the ability to diversify their portfolio with a single investment.

- REIT: A real estate investment trust (REIT) is a company that owns or operates income-producing real estate, such as apartments, hotels, or office buildings. Investors in REITs own a share of the income and appreciation generated by the real estate held in the trust.

Initially, the 401(k) was created to allow employers to offer their workers a tax-deferred retirement savings plan and make contributions on their behalf. Over time, the 401(k) has become one of the most popular retirement savings plans in the US, with the majority of employers providing some type of 401(k) plan to their employees. The plan has undergone various changes and enhancements, including the addition of catch-up contributions for those over fifty and the option to transfer 401(k) funds to other retirement accounts.

Investing has been made to appear complicated, with many barriers in place that make it seem more difficult than it needs to be. In the past, employers provided retirement income to their workers through pension plans or defined benefit plans. However, in the 1980s, the 401(k) or defined contribution plan emerged, shifting the responsibility of investing and saving for retirement from the employer to the employee. The

government incentivized investing by offering tax breaks for
401(k) plans and other retirement accounts like the Roth IRA
and IRA, as it doesn't want people to solely depend on Social
Security in retirement. Although Social Security exists, it's
insufficient to cover all expenses in retirement, so individuals are encouraged to save for retirement through investing.

While the shift to 401(k) plans allowed employees to have
more control over their retirement savings and provided tax
benefits, it also meant that they were solely responsible for
ensuring that they saved enough for their retirement. This
transition also brought about barriers for employees, such as
enrolling in the plan, selecting the right investments, and determining how much to invest to ensure they have enough
money when they retire. Given the volatility of the stock
market, constrained income, and inflation driving up the cost
of living, it's no wonder that many people put off the idea of
investing or don't invest enough, especially considering the
already overwhelming number of daily decisions they face
and the perceived limitations on their income.

If you're anything like me, it's challenging enough sometimes to foresee or figure out what we want for dinner so it's
unrealistic to expect most people to accurately forecast our financial needs and goals for twenty to fifty years in the future.

If you contribute to a 401(k) or other type of company-
sponsored retirement account, you are already an investor
and have investments, but it may not feel that way since the
concept of what society says an investor looks like seems out
of reach or confusing. You may feel like in order to be a true
investor, you should be investing in complicated or more advanced assets or that you should be in front of a computer

researching companies, reading quarterly reports, and day trading.

While investments such as cryptocurrency and real estate may appear attractive and more official due to their complexity and perceived status, they typically require more upfront capital and knowledge to understand them. However, simpler and more established investment strategies exist that can lead to success as an investor. They may not be as exciting or seemingly as sexy as some of the other forms of investing or get rich quick schemes you hear about, but they work and don't even require a lot of effort or money to start.

For many people, investing—and especially the idea of investing in retirement accounts—feels like having invisible money, or not having that money at all. You can't hold it, touch it, or spend. When you could be spending that money on things you want today, it's easy to see why you haven't been excited about funneling your precious dollars into some account you don't understand or connect with. This kind of wealth is low-key, so not only does it feel invisible to you, but it's invisible to others. Others can't see that you have $100,000 in your 401(k) like they can see that you are driving a $100,000 car.

THE MAGIC OF INDEX FUNDS

My favorite vehicle or investment is the Index Fund. Index funds are a type of mutual fund that tracks a market index. The index fund mirrors the returns of the market index it is tracking. Some popular market indexes are the S&P 500 which is the Standard & Poor's 500, a stock market index that tracks and measures the value of the top 500 largest public companies listed on the NY Stock Exchange. Companies such as Amazon, Apple, Walmart, etc., can all be found on the NY Stock Exchange; so when you buy an index fund that tracks the S&P 500, you are buying a piece of all 500 of those companies. If one company doesn't do well or falls out of the top 500, it is replaced by another company. Your money and return doesn't depend on just one company, it relies on the collective and average. Essentially buying an index fund allows you to ride the average returns of the top 500 companies over time and while the entire market will go up and down, as a long-term investor you are keeping your money invested for a ten- to fifty-year-plus length of time and can ride out any market declines. Over time and since its inception in 1928, the S&P 500 has had a historical average return of 9.81%. Some years the return might be -5%, and sometimes the returns can be +20%. All that matters is that you are invested in it and along for the ride in the long term.

COMPARING RISK AND RETURN

Take time to compare investing in index funds to investing in a single stock. Sure, it's possible to select individual companies and stocks that you believe will perform well, and you may even choose well. However, this approach involves taking on more concentrated risk, whereas investing in the overall market and passively waiting for returns on average can be a more efficient strategy. The average return, low work, and low effort aren't the only reasons I like index funds. Index funds' fees are also typically low because they are not actively managed funds—meaning you don't have to pay overhead for people to maintain and manage the account. On average, index funds have a management fee of 0.06%, whereas actively managed funds average 0.47%. While that might not seem like a big difference, those fees can add up. For example, on a portfolio that grows to $1,128,612 over a period of thirty years, a 0.47% management fee equals $133,963, and a 0.06% management fee equals $18,042—a $115,921 difference. Unless your actively managed fund outperforms the passively managed index fund—and historically, 90% of actively managed funds have underperformed the S&P Composite 1500 over the last twenty years—then the extra fees aren't worth it.

I'm not saying you can't have actively managed funds as part of your portfolio or you can't work with a financial advisor or investment firm to manage your portfolio, *but* a less costly and easier way to start building your investment portfolio is to open an investment account on your own at a brokerage firm and buy low-cost index funds.

The dilemma is that beginner investors or those with limited capital would benefit more from opening investment accounts and choosing low-cost index funds or target date funds as starting investments, which can be easily accessed through online investment companies such as Vanguard and Fidelity. However, due to their lack of experience and fear of making mistakes, they may be more likely to either avoid investing altogether or opting for more complex and expensive options.

WHY INVESTING IN A RETIREMENT ACCOUNT IS IMPORTANT

If you couldn't tell already, I'm a big advocate of investing with tax-advantaged retirement accounts. The benefits are plenty and while there may be some things you'll need to be mindful of (fees and the difference between actively managed and self-managed accounts, the age you can take withdrawal, and penalty for early withdrawals), if you're on this journey for the long haul, then it's a smart, stealthy, steady path to building and obtaining wealth. You can still choose to invest in other types of assets and accounts, but doing this as the basic first step gives you the ability and confidence to take more risk in other areas. It provides you with that safety net to fall back on since you are building wealth the slow and predictable way. It's like knowing your parents will always allow you to live with them if you have a hard time in the real world, you may be inclined to take more risk knowing that you always have a safe place to land. Or better yet, it's like knowing you have that delicious leftover meal in the fridge or home-cooked meal at home, but you find yourself out at a restaurant. You can order the dish you typically order or take a risk and order something that you've never had before that looks delicious. Knowing you have something amazing at home to eat, you may be more willing to take a risk and order something new. If you don't like it, you can eat your tasty leftovers when you get home. If you love it, you've added a new dish to your rotation. It's a win either way. That's how I want you to view investing. You can create a solid nest egg through your regular boring retirement and taxable investment accounts using index funds. Take care of the basic stuff first and then you can put yourself in a better position to take more risk and increase your probability of reaching your financial goals. In the case of reaching financial independence and being able to retire early, once you're on this path and building your investment accounts, the chances of you being able to retire at the standard retirement age has increased exponentially so that you can take more detours, change routes, switch jobs, and spend more in the moment on the things you enjoy.

INVESTING BENEFITS

You save money on taxes

Remember when you invest in pre-tax retirement accounts, contributions are deducted from your gross income before taxes are calculated, which lowers your taxable income in the year. This allows you to potentially save on taxes now, even though you will have to pay taxes on the money when you withdraw it during retirement. The idea is that you'll likely be in a lower tax bracket during retirement compared to your working years, so you'll pay less in taxes overall. (Since we have no idea where tax rates will be in the future, this is an estimated theory, but the general guidance).

Instead of giving Uncle Sam more of your money today, you get to keep more of it and put it away for yourself. If you've been one to complain about the government taking too much in taxes out of your paycheck, investing in pre-tax retirement accounts is your opportunity to have less taxes taken out.

Investing now creates a comfortable cushion for your future self

When I first entered the workforce full-time, I was solely focused on my present financial situation and neglected to think about my future. I gave little consideration to the money I was handing over to the government in taxes, instead of investing it in myself. Do you want to end up like those who have to work well into their golden years just to make ends meet, or rely on others for financial assistance? I certainly don't. While it may be difficult to think about your future self fifteen to thirty years from now, remember where you were a decade ago. Would you have made different choices if you knew then what you know now? Time waits for no one, and before you know it, you'll be looking back on your life. The question is, will you have set yourself up for financial success by taking the initiative to invest or will you be struggling to make ends meet?

Even though you are investing for the long term, it's an asset to you right now

People tend to falsely assume that investing in retirement accounts means not being able to access that money until twenty to thirty years from now, but in reality, the money in your investment accounts is still your money and you can actually access it, though in most cases with a fee. While I will always encourage you to keep your money in the account and pretend it doesn't exist for the sake of allowing it to grow and accumulate to its maximum potential, you can access the money you need. If you've contributed to a Roth IRA, which is referred to as the principal amount, you have the flexibility to withdraw those contributed funds at any time without incurring penalties or taxes since you have already paid taxes on them when you initially deposited the money. For example, if you contributed $20,000 to your Roth IRA over the span of five years and your account grew to $29,000, the $9,000 difference represents the return on interest or growth, while the original $20,000 can be accessed without penalties or taxes whenever needed.

I know it feels contradictory or confusing because on one hand I'm asking you to invest your money and not pay attention to it, almost forget it exists so that you can allow it to grow and not obsess over daily or monthly returns. On the other hand, I want you to consider it and be fully aware of it so you can prioritize investing in it and be excited about having it. But two things can be true at the same time, you can hold space for these two attitudes but switch which one needs to be more at the forefront to help you when necessary. You can view your retirement investments as a long-term wealth strategy that you prioritize even if you have no intention of using the money right away, and see it as your short-term freedom strategy because it still can act like a cushion and investing in it today allows you to feel comfortable enough to also spend today on the things that you care about.

Don't think of it as your retirement account; the name in itself doesn't invoke much inspiration since many people don't think they can retire. Retirement has always meant a time far away when what many people want to do is just simply enjoy today. You would be better served to view or rebrand your retirement account as your financial independence account.

Imagine how much more confident you would feel in your decisions today if you knew that you were either on track or working to get on track to have enough for your traditional retirement and for your desired FI goals? That means you have enough in your current investment accounts to reach your goals in your future and you are content with your ongoing contributions that you plan to make. That means any other money you bring in is yours to do with as you please. You can spend without guilt or hesitation on whatever you want now because your future is set.

I had the confidence to quit my job and go full-time into my business because I knew I had long-term investments that I could rely on. Today, I am able to enjoy my lifestyle, like going on vacations and having brunch with my friends, because I feel a sense of security with my money. It doesn't mean that I don't have moments of fear and questions around money like "do I really have enough?" or "should I be investing more?"—but I am able to reassure myself and walk back from the edge that is common when it comes to the what-ifs because I know I have savings and investments that will carry me through. And even when I think of the worst-case scenario, like what if all my money and monetary assets were to be taken away, I go back to belief in my biggest asset, myself. I know that I have my brain, mindset, intangible resources, and community to be able to figure something out if it all goes away.

Imagine being able to comfortably take the trips you want, go out to eat when you want, put your kids in the pricey summer camp today or in one to five years—all while not having to worry about your future because you have taken care of your long-term investments already?

HABITS FOR SAVING AND INVESTING

Make saving for your goals and investing for retirement automatic. Set up direct monthly contributions to your savings account from your paycheck. The contributions from your paycheck to sponsored retirement accounts are typically direct and automatic and are usually set up through your employer through your HR department or online employee retirement portal.

To ensure consistent contributions to your Traditional IRA, Roth IRA, and taxable investment accounts established with brokerage firms, set up automatic monthly transfers from your bank account. Choose an amount that fits your budget so that you don't have to make manual contributions. If you have additional funds available in your gap and want to contribute more, you can do so manually, but at least you'll have a regular amount automatically contributed every month to your investment account.

IMPROVING MINDSET AROUND INVESTING

I understand why you may have been hesitant before or still have hesitations about investing, but because it's such an integral part in your success to reach financial independence, I want to help you move closer to getting started so here are some potential questions or objections you may still have that I want to address:

I can't access the money right away, so what's the point?

You are creating a nest egg for yourself and your future self will thank you, but you can access your money if you need to but may pay some penalties and taxes depending on the circumstances. You can access your Roth IRA contributions at any time without any penalty. Early retirees often utilize a strategy called Roth IRA ladders to access their funds before the typical age of fifty-nine and a half. This involves transferring money from pre-tax retirement accounts, such as Traditional IRA and 401(k) into a Roth IRA and paying ordinary taxes on the converted amount. You have to wait five years to withdraw that money and then you don't have to pay a penalty on it. Each conversion will stand on its own and people typically do it year after year so that when the first conversion meets the five-year waiting period, they can begin to withdraw money they'll take as income. Also, it's not necessarily about using the money in these accounts right now but the security and freedom that having money in these accounts allow you. The benefit to having funds in your retirement account allows you to spend more money now on the things you want and need to live a comfortable life.

I don't have enough money to invest right now.

Every little bit counts—$150 invested every month can turn into $100,000 in twenty years (assuming a $2,000 starting amount and 8% return). Besides, if you begin to work on and implement the other components of the FI formula that we talked about so far (mindset, expenses, habits, and income), you will begin to see more increases in your gap and have the additional money you need to invest.

I would rather use my money now to live life, I may die tomorrow.

True (I hope not, though), but what if you don't? You may very well live until you're old and gray and then what? We can't predict the future but we can do our best to set ourselves up for success. And there's a way to balance both enjoying the now and setting yourself up for a fruitful future. Maybe you don't invest as intensely or aggressively now and take a slower approach to your journey to FI so that you can focus on more of your lifestyle goals and discretionary spending, and that's okay too.

What about the fees?

If you are investing in a company-sponsored retirement account, a 401(k) through your job, then there may be fees that are unavoidable. You can do your due diligence and check out the fees associated with each asset class or investment you have and compare them and may find there is a better lower-cost investment option that provides a similar return. If you find that your company simply does not provide you with reasonable investment choices without high fees, it still makes sense to invest. Reach out to your plan administrator or HR to talk about having more options.

Additionally, when opening a taxable brokerage investment account or a Roth or Traditional IRA independently, without the involvement of an employer, or as a business owner setting up a retirement account, you have greater autonomy to choose the brokerage company and lower-fee investments.

It will take too long to see the results I want to achieve; I need to take more risks.

Investing and risk go hand in hand. You may be underestimating how fast you can start to accumulate wealth doing it the steady and slow way. With compounding interest, your first $100,000 may take ten years, but your next $100,000 may only take 6 years, the next $100,000 4 years, and so on.

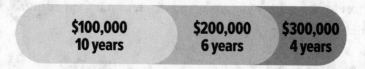

1 2 3 4 5 6 7 8 9 10 11 12 13 14 15 16 17 18 19 20 YEARS

Assuming starting balance of $1k and 500 monthly contributions
at 8% monthly compounding interest rate

I'm young; I have time to figure it out.

Youth is on your side. If you are in your teens or twenties, getting started now allows you to be able to do less work as you get older. The earlier you start the better, because your money has more time to compound and grow. For instance, if you have a longer investing horizon, the time you have to invest, then you can invest $215 a month to accumulate $1,000,000 over a forty-year time span vs. a scenario where you have only a twenty-year horizon, and you'll need to invest $1,500 a month to accumulate $1,000,000.

HOW MUCH YOU NEED TO INVEST MONTHLY TO GET TO $1 MILLION

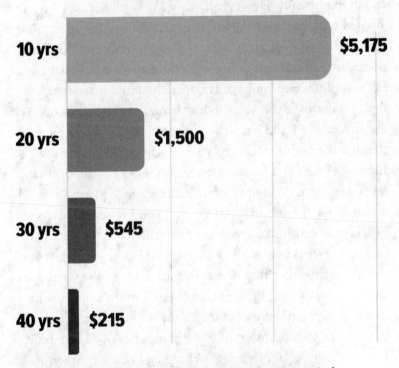

$ PER MONTH 9% RETURN

10 yrs	$5,175
20 yrs	$1,500
30 yrs	$545
40 yrs	$215

I'm too old and it's too late for whatever I do starting now to make a difference.

You're never too old to start. Not even in your forties or fifties. You could well live for another thirty to forty years. That's another lifetime to live and get started.

Let's look at the case of Leilani, who was on episode 270 of the podcast. Leilani learned about the FIRE movement at forty-two years old, in the middle of a self-proclaimed midlife

crisis. Leilani didn't have a clear picture of what she was seek-
ing, but she knew she needed a change, something different
from the norm. Following her curiosity, Leilani started listening to personal finance podcasts. At first, many stories she came
across about achieving FI centered around real estate investing
and living frugally. However, Leilani knew those paths weren't
aligned with her desired lifestyle goals. She kept an open mind
and continued exploring, which led her to podcasts like mine,
books, and stories that began to resonate with her. Leilani and
her husband were doing well financially, and she had increased
her income over the years, but it wasn't until she discovered
the magic of FI and embarked on her intentional FI journey
that her life and finances truly transformed. She made investing in her 401(k) a priority, increasing her contribution, and
started to aggressively pay off her mortgage. At first, her goal
was to leave her job in seven years. Then her seven-year plan
quickly turned into a five-year plan, then a three-year plan,
and before she knew it, she was able to quit her job in just two
years, much earlier than she anticipated. Once she started, as
she said, "dabbling in the possibilities," more opportunities
came to her. Leilani embraced her entrepreneurial spirit and
turned her passion into profit by starting her own bartending
business and began offering coaching and consulting services.
While she has not reached complete FI just yet, she considers
herself Journeyer stage 4, work flexible.

**I don't want to help make someone else richer or
participate in this capitalist system any more than
I have to.**

I understand. The system isn't fair, but we either have the
choice to remain idle and be further marginalized or actively

engage in the most constructive way possible to provide ourselves and future generations with a better opportunity. By increasing our wealth, we can contribute more to support causes and individuals in need. We don't have to perpetuate the problems and become another cog in a system that helps to keep it running, but we can improve our economic standard and use our money to create the impact and change we want to see.

You also have the option to invest in ESG (Environmental, Social, and Governance) funds. ESG investments or funds are those that consider environmental, social, and governance factors in the investment process. These factors are used to evaluate the sustainability and ethical impact of companies and investments. ESG investing has become increasingly popular in recent years as investors seek to align their investments with their values and promote sustainability and social responsibility.

I love what I do and don't ever see myself retiring.

If that's true then you've accomplished what many are still looking for. You've technically cracked the code because I believe we all want to love and enjoy what we do. Finding something you love and that earns you a living is the goal. But you still want to have options, because in the same way that your opinion or interest has changed from those of the person you were ten years ago, your mind can change about what you want in the future. You may want the ability to take a break, travel, start a family, do something completely different and starting now will give you the ability to have the option to do that. Besides, no job is guaranteed.

INVESTING BASED ON JOURNEYER STAGE

In this section, I'll give you some guidelines on where you should be investing based on your Journeyer level. The amount you'll be able to invest to reach FI will be dependent on your goals and the six components resulting in your gap, but the following will give you an idea of where to start.

JOURNEYER STAGE	INVESTING STRATEGY
Explorer	Not unless you are already investing.
Cadet	Yes, up until company match if available and as you create more of a gap split extra cash up between investing and paying off debt.
Aviator	Primary focus is on investing.
Commander	The intensity of your investments depends on your goals.
Captain	Maintain or, if desired, grow your investments.

Explorer: In this stage you're primarily focused on getting to a level of stability. If you are already investing in your company 401(k) or retirement plan, keep doing it but modestly. Focus your efforts on covering your expenses with your income.

Cadet: In this stage you're primarily focused on paying off consumer debt, but you can still invest. You should invest at least up to your 401(k) company match if they offer it so that you can boost your investments. Then decide how you want to split your gap between debt payoff and investments.

Aviator: In this stage you're working on building security through asset accumulation and investing. Since you have paid off all of your consumer debt, you can focus your efforts more on investing.

Commander: In this stage you have some work flexibility but still may want to invest so that you can reach your FI goals and build your investment account cushion. You can decide how intense you want to be based on your FI goals.

Captain: In this stage you've reached complete FI and have enough money invested to sustain your lifestyle. You can decide to stop investing altogether or continue to invest.

These are only suggestions, and everyone's situation will be different. The amount you can invest is relative to your income and expenses. For instance, if you have a mid-to-high income on paper but are unable to maximize your retirement account or contribute to your investments as much as you would like, it may be due to your current high expenses that cannot be reduced. These expenses may include taking care of extended family, having young children in daycare (or simply having children), dealing with high levels of debt repayment or a costly mortgage/rent, living in a high-cost area, or managing medical expenses. All these circumstances are valid reasons why you may not be able to invest the maximum amount you want to in your investment accounts. Still, it's important to make conscious choices about your priorities. For example, you may choose not to invest more money right now because there's something else in your budget that's important to you or you're unwilling to change. Making this choice means taking ownership of your circumstances.

Part 3: Executing Your Financial Independence Plan Checklist

Step 1: Optimize Expenses

- [ ] Evaluate Your Expenses

- [ ] Identify Expenses To Eliminate & Reduce

- [ ] Identify Expenses To Increase

- [ ] Improve Mindset & Habits Around Expenses

- [ ] Take Action on Optimizing Expenses

- [ ] Call Service Providers & Negotiate Rates

- [ ] Downsize or Eliminate Costly Expenses if Possible

- [ ] Eliminate or Reduce Daily or Recurring Expenses

- [ ] Spend More in Areas That Bring You Joy or Are Helpful

- [ ] Put Money Saved From Optimizing Expenses Towards Financial & Lifestyle Goals

Step 2: Increase Income

- [ ] Evaluate Your Income

- [ ] Identify Ways To Increase Your Income Through Current Job

- [ ] Identify Ways To Increase Your Income Through Other Job/ Careers

- [ ] Identify Ways To Increase Your Income Through Side Hustles & Entrepreneurship

- [ ] Improve Mindset & Habits Around Income

- [ ] Take Action on Increasing Income

- [ ] Negotiate Salary at Current Job

- [ ] Interview At Other Jobs & Negotiate New Salary

- [ ] Execute Side Hustle & Entrepreneurship Ideas

- [ ] Put Additional Money Earned From Increasing Income Towards Financial & Lifestyle Goals

Step 3: Pay Down Liabilities/Debt

- [ ] Evaluate Your Liabilities

- [ ] Create A Debt Payoff Plan

- [ ] Improve Mindset & Habits Around Debt

- [ ] Take Action on Decreasing Debt

- [ ] Include Debt Payoff Plan in Budget

- [ ] Set up Automatic Debt Payments

- [ ] Increase Debt Payments When Possible

Step 4: Increase Assets

☐   Evaluate Your Assets

☐   Identify Savings Goals

☐   Identify Investing Goals

☐   Create a Saving & Investing Plan

☐   Improve Mindset & Habits Around Increasing Assets

☐   Take Action on Increasing Assets

☐   Include Saving & Investing Goals in Budget

☐   Open Up High-Yield Savings Account

☐   Invest Up to Company Match for 401(K)

☐   Open Roth IRA

☐   Open Taxable Account

☐   Increase Contributions to Pre-Tax Retirement Accounts & Taxable Accounts

☐   Set Up Automatic Contributions to Investment Accounts

PART 4:

ENJOYING THE JOURNEY

13

THE IMPORTANCE OF STAYING FOCUSED AND CONSISTENT ON THE PATH TO FINANCIAL INDEPENDENCE

Now that you have developed a basic plan along with strategies to enhance the components (FI) formula to achieve your specific financial and lifestyle objectives, one question arises: Now what? The duration of your journey to FI can vary greatly depending on various factors, including your starting point and unforeseen circumstances that may crop up in the future. It's important to acknowledge that attaining FI might span several decades based on these variables.

Trying to find an optimal or perfect order for how you should execute and pursue financial independence in terms of what you focus on first and do first with your life is a valid pursuit but also an unrealistic one. That's because while you may set out to do things in the perfect order and make plans for the future, your circumstances and preferences will and can change. The moments and people that make up your life can't be quantified, optimized, or organized in a spreadsheet.

The feelings and joy you want to experience may not always fit into the plan you initially set out for yourself and that's okay. The beauty of creating the initial plan is to know that it is just that, an initial plan, a home base to come back to, a check-in, but you have full control to deviate from that plan as necessary. When I first started my journey, I thought working at my corporate job and aggressively saving and investing my salary would be my way out. I'd just need to sacrifice seven years of my life in order to reach my financial goals. But a couple years into the grind of the job, with my side hustle at the time, *Journey to Launch*, commuting, and growing a family, I knew that life could not be sustainable. At that point, it didn't matter how much I was able to save and invest from my paycheck so I had to figure out a new plan that would allow me to enjoy my life. The priority was no longer how much I could save or optimize for money, but optimizing for time and freedom and joy. So we switched our strategy and started preparing for me to leave my corporate job. Instead of saving and investing money in investment accounts, we started saving money to help cover our household expenses as I prepared to make the exit. Because I had my initial plan in place and a forecast of what we wanted to save and invest to reach financial independence, playing around with different scenarios to show how not investing for a few years would impact our future plans allowed me to alleviate some of the unknowns that came with leaving my job. The worst-case scenario of not making enough money with *Journey to Launch* and having to go back to get a nine-to-five if my entrepreneurial pursuits didn't work was not as scary because I knew I could withstand the worst of it. Fear mostly comes from the unknown and because our futures are unpredictable, it can be hard to plan ahead. The what-ifs and endless outcomes can paralyze you from making a decision because you want to make the right decision. Either you avoid thinking about it or overthink to the point where you do nothing.

THE IMPORTANCE OF COMMUNITY AND SOCIAL CAPITAL

Being around other people who think the same can create an echo chamber and that is not always a good thing. A lot of us are in echo chambers by default while growing up because we have no choice or autonomy over where we can live or who our family is or where we go to school. We are literally placed in a specific environment, and because it's all we hear and see we initially think that environment standard is the norm. As we begin to grow up and get access to books and TV, and are given more space to roam the world rather than just the neighborhood store we begin to be exposed to other things.

You can either choose to maintain the status quo for the illusion of comfort or face the necessary challenges to bring about the desired change. Consider whether the feeling you perceive as comfort is genuine or if it is simply a result of being accustomed to the discomfort and unhappiness that have become your new norm.

We often talk about capital in terms of money, but there are other forms of capital that are important and necessary for you to build for a successful and happy life. The one I'll focus on for this outside of economic capital is the concept of social capital.

Robert Putnam, author of *Bowling Alone: The Collapse and Revival of American Community*, describes social capital as "connections among individuals—social networks and the norms of reciprocity and trustworthiness that arise from them."

Social capital can be cultivated and earned through relationships formed through formal organizations and groups like churches, PTA, etc., or informal networks and relationships like having dinner with friends and family. Even just knowing your neighbor's name or them knowing who you are is a positive form of social capital.

Social capital can be seen or demonstrated through being able to reach out to your old college network or alumni group to inquire about job opportunities or your neighbors keeping an eye on your house for you while you are away on vacation.

We all need social capital, and if you are not born into wealth or don't have a lot of economic capital to begin with—which is most of us—social capital is vital to your success and happiness, both financially and otherwise. Social capital also encompasses your relationships with family, friends, neighbors, and colleagues. Your goal may be to have enough money to choose what you want to do with your time, but ultimately, how will you spend your time once it's yours to control? Many of us want to spend it with people we enjoy and love. You don't need money to build this kind of social capital to improve your quality of your life.

Feeling connected to others who can support you on your journey is important. It's about more than surrounding yourself with people who are into finances and can talk budgets with you. While it's important to be part of that group, you also need people and support systems that allow you to feel connected and experience a sense of community.

You have to join groups or communities where your stretch or big goals are their actual everyday reality. Have a goal of becoming a top earner, you'll benefit from knowing people who are well paid. Want to become a successful entrepreneur? Your chances of succeeding at becoming one will improve greatly by knowing and having relationships with successful entrepreneurs. If you surround yourself with people who have fallen into the status quo way of thinking and doing things, how can you expect to break through to your desired level of success and your FI goal? You're less likely to know what options and opportunities exist or see what's possible when you're not exposed to it. The beautiful thing about this is that these relationships or connections don't have to be in person or even through knowing the person in real life. It can be hard to gain access to the people you truly aspire to be inspired by, but just because you're not physically in the room doesn't mean you can't benefit from their energy and knowledge.

There are tons of podcasts, online blogs, and social media accounts that you can find that can encourage you and help you stay motivated. When I had my one and a half to sometimes two-hour commute each way, I'd listen to various podcasts. It was in my car and through listening to podcasts that I learned about how others were pursuing financial independence. I listened to people tell stories of how they started their businesses or traveled the world and it opened up my world to a new way of thinking. On my dreariest of days I knew that I could read or listen to something that could help encourage me to keep moving forward. I didn't have to know these people in real life to learn from them. If I liked a person's interview on a podcast and they talked about their business or blog, I'd seek them out and read more about them. I listened to their other interviews, checked out some of the resources they cited as helpful.

My first glimpse into seeing that I could actually make money doing *Journey to Launch* full-time was when I met and became group chat friends with Bola Sunkubi of Clever Girl Finance. Bola was just a few steps ahead of us in terms of her own business journey, but at the time to me, she seemed to be miles ahead. She had already established her brand Clever Girl Finance and it was one of the standouts in the personal finance space. At the time she had about 34,000 followers on Instagram, which might as well have been one million followers to me. I probably had 120 followers back then. For about a year, we'd talk in the group chat about our businesses. I was still working at my corporate job and didn't have the intention of going into my business full-time, but watching Bola come up with plans to grow her business and earn money from it opened me up to a new possibility. She was earning money in her business and she was a mom, a Black woman, and everyday regular girl just like me. I started to observe others from afar in the online business personal finance space. People who were also similar to but different from me. They had amazing debt payoff stories, were starting podcasts, were becoming coaches to help people with their money issues, were working with brands and writing or doing work that earned them money. Not soon after I started to think about *Journey to Launch* as a potential business, I learned about a conference for personal finance content creators and business owners. Many of the bloggers I followed or podcasters I listened to, or people like me who were just starting out, were part of this community. If I wanted to see that this could be my reality, going to conferences and becoming part of the community was top priority. I had to be in the room where it happened, to see up close what could be done, and that's what I did. In addition to going to that money conference, I went to my first podcast conference the year I started my own podcast. Being able to connect with other creators, business owners, and podcasters in person really changed things for me. I knew for real that this could be my reality.

"IF ONE CAN DO IT, YOU CAN BE TWO. IF NONE HAS DONE IT, YOU CAN BE ONE."

If you surround yourself with people only impressed by material things or things that are contradictory to your goals—e.g., praise for buying a car, expensive items, or liabilities that sparkle—then you will want to continue to get your approval from and look for admiration through those activities. You have to *also* find people that will cheer for you paying off debt, saving money as loud and as proudly as the other crowd. It will be like you're living in the world as Clark Kent, looking average, where people may underestimate your abilities, potentially look you over, when in reality you're Superman fighting and beating the bad guys every night. Finding a supportive community of like-minded individuals can make a significant difference in staying motivated and feeling appreciated. This group of fellow "undercover superheroes" can help cheer you on as you tackle challenges such as paying off credit card debt or increasing your 401(k) contributions, giving you the recognition and encouragement you need to keep pushing forward. You don't have to remove yourself or materialistic people from your life, but you have to have a variety of outside validation. People you can celebrate with when you pay off debt, start the side hustle, and the people who can celebrate you when you buy your dream car or take that once in a lifestyle vacation. The point is you should have support from people who can say "#goals" or "good job" for your financial accomplishments, just as much as they celebrate your lifestyle accomplishments and it's fine if these are different groups.

On the path to achieving your goals, there may be many moments where your accomplishments are not recognized by others or may seem insignificant. This can lead to feelings of frustration or discouragement, but it's important to celebrate and take pride in your victories, no matter how small they may seem.

DOING THIS WITH A PARTNER

Since we are talking about the importance of social capital which is all built on relationships, what about the relationships closest to you that will impact how you move forward on your journey? How to manage them and relate to romantic partners, friends, and family is a big part of your journey. The financial independence journey is a solo venture and yet as we talked about you can't do it alone and if you want to enjoy it, navigating conversations, situations, and life with the people closest to you is important. To ignore the fact that having a partner, children, or family that depend on you are not big factors would be a mistake.

For Ledo and Shameka who were on episode 139 of the podcast getting on the same page required honest conversations. Shameka was the one primarily taking care of their finances. It wasn't until Ledo found out about FI through a podcast that he realized how much more they could be doing and accomplishing with their money. When he first brought the idea to Shameka, she said she felt a little offended. The method they had worked, she thought, so why did they need to change it. They paid their bills on time, had a manageable amount of debt, and were still able to do things like go on vacation. But once she saw Ledo's excitement and how dedicated and serious he was to seeing his vision through action, she said she couldn't help but get on board. Once getting on the same page and becoming more intentional with their goals to reach FI, they were able to pay $32,000 in debt and built $100,000 in net worth.

If your partner is at first apprehensive, defensive, or even offended when they first hear about the concept of FI and what needs to change in order to accomplish it, offer them space and grace to share their emotions. Explain your vision that you see for your family, but give them just as much room to add to that vision too. It's important to make sure that they feel like this is a joint goal that you both are working toward. You don't have to think the exact same way or have the same goals, but you should have a common purpose and game plan that incorporates your joint and individual goals. This is even more important when you have children because your actions no longer just affect the two of you.

Our family finances drastically improved once Woody and I got on the same page. We went from unintentionally spending and living in the moment to purposely planning and investing for our future. Our family savings rate substantially increased once we came together and started working toward our future goals. While Woody isn't a natural spender, he's also not a numbers guy. I'm the planner and self-designated CFO of our family. When it came time to think of ways to rapidly increase our saving and investing rate so that I could "retire early," I was met with some skepticism. "You want to do what, and how and where, with my money? Girl, bye…" Okay, he didn't say it like that, but I felt he was thinking that when I approached him with my brilliant idea of rapidly increasing our savings rate so that I could retire by the time I reached forty years old. The plan I wanted to present him was essentially this:

Let's increase our overall saving and investing rate. This means that you will have to increase your pre-tax retirement contributions from just 7% to almost 50%. Your take-home pay will be cut in half, but the good news is, I'll get to retire early…"

Yeah, no. That wasn't going to work. I was going to have to approach the situation completely differently in order to get him on board. As I started to learn more about topics or hear interesting stories, I began sharing them with him. Things I knew he would relate to, like a teacher becoming a millionaire or an ex-athlete story about living on a small percentage of their salary. When you begin to have conversations with your partner, share things you truly find to be interesting or thought-provoking. You should be genuine in your reason for sending the information. Let them form their own opinion from the information you share. Remember, the goal here is not to manipulate your partner, but to have them willfully join you on the financial journey. In the very beginning, Woody and I also began having family planning/budgeting meetings. After having a few casual discussions about your goals and finances, it may be time to sit down and have a family planning meeting. The purpose of this meeting is to plan out how you can realistically accomplish individual and family goals.

At this meeting you can: set goals, review or create a budget, and develop a plan that you both agree on. You'll need to get your partner to buy in; they need to have a stake in the plan. They will feel some ownership and commitment to the goals you create together. You also have to be willing to be flexible. Your goals may change or your partner may change their mind. Your financial situation also may change which can force you to reconsider your goals. Ideally, you two should be periodically checking in on your goals and progress to make sure you still want the same things. You can help avoid resentment as long as there is open communication where both parties feel free to express concerns without backlash or judgment. If your partner has a completely different goal or want in life, hear them out and figure out a way to make accomplishing both your goals possible. For example, Woody would love to have a luxury car and while I'd be content with not having a luxury car, it's important to him. I have to be willing to listen to what he wants even if it's not something I want and see how it can fit into our FI plan. I am willing to push back my retirement date by a few months or work a little harder to save up for it. The carrot for me is early retirement and FI, the carrot for him is a nice luxury car. It's not up to me to judge his goals because they are different from mine.

Another important way we made incremental changes was that we didn't jump from contributing 6% to 48% of Woody's gross income to pre-tax retirement accounts overnight. We started gradually increasing his contributions every month. One month it was 7%, the next month we bumped it to 8% and so on. I also reiterated to Woody that everything was reversible and we could always reduce the percent if things got too tight or if he was uncomfortable. After a couple months of gradually increasing the percentage, Woody came to me and said, let's just bump it to 50%.

It's not uncommon for one person in the relationship to be more involved or leading in the family finances. Usually one person feels more comfortable doing it and the other partner is happy to release the reins and let the other person navigate. I think it's important that you let go of the expectation that your partner has to share the same exact level of enthusiasm or involvement moving forward once you do start the journey together. While you should be on the same page and it's great if you have the same exact intensity, it's not realistic that this will be the case in every relationship. To this day, Woody is content to let me steer the rocket as he really is not as interested in the day to day managing of our finances and I've released any expectation that he needs to be involved if he doesn't want to be. As long as there are regular check-ins on how each other is feeling, full transparency of where you are financially, and the partner who is less involved by choice feels they have equal say and control then it's okay to not break what is already working.

If you feel like there is an unfair power dynamic or lack of transparency around your finances then having someone take more of the lead on them wouldn't be best as it may cause more issues. Also when it comes to how a couple handles finances you may find that you want to keep your finances completely separate and only combine your finances for shared goals, which is fine too. You have to find the financial setup that works for the both of you—key words—it needs to work for and be agreed to by both parties.

WHAT ABOUT THE CHILDREN?

Children are as expensive or inexpensive as you want them to be. Of course, there are unavoidable costs that come with raising children, the most costly one being daycare in the early years, but you can be intentional about what matters to you when it comes to spending in the other areas of food, clothes, extracurricular activities, vacations, etc.

Be realistic about the lifestyle you want to give your children and what it means for your FI goals. We value experiences and extracurricular activities when it comes to how we spend on our children and make trade-offs when it comes to buying clothes or spending on everyday smaller purchases for them. That means we budget a lot more money in our spending for vacations, events, and sports activities than other areas for them. We don't buy more than we need when it comes to clothing and I try to limit our after-school ice cream purchases from the ice cream truck—hello, one Mister Softee cone with sprinkles runs us about $4 each, multiply by 3 and every day after-school stops at the park with ice cream add up:

$4 x 3= $12 a day, $12 x 5 = $60 a week, and $60 x 4 = $240 a month—assuming we gave into their every request for "can we get some ice cream from the ice cream truck?!"

If you have different priorities than me, that's fine too. There is no judgment on how you want to spend your money on your own children.

While I'd like to be able to give them everything they want, we just can't; our income has limits. Limits are not necessarily a bad thing. Most parents, including myself, aspire to offer their children an enhanced lifestyle compared to their own childhood experiences. The ultimate goal is to enable your children to surpass your own achievements and have greater opportunities in life.

When I think back at how much my mom was able to do with me and for me with a limited income and barely any help, I'm amazed. I was in swimming and gymnastics classes and even though I didn't always have the newest Air Jordans (she did buy me one pair in high school) I never felt like I had less than others. What I lacked in clothes or vacations, she made up with love. Her confidence and support in me really gave me the ability to thrive the way I did and do now. If you can't financially give your children the things you want because of the lack of money, know that investing in them is not just through dollars. You can invest in them with words, affection, and love which in the long run mean more than any pair of Jordans could.

When it comes to your financial goals, just like a flight attendant says before your plane takes off, in case of an emergency, put on your mask first before helping others and in this case that even means when thinking about your finances: make sure you're financially okay first. If you're not on track for standard retirement or have near or immediate goals that are more beneficial for your family, prioritize that over thinking about investing or saving for your kids' future. I'll have parents ask me how they should go about putting money away for their kids' college fund and I ask them if they are investing for themselves and they say no. You may mean well by thinking you are putting your kids before you because as a parent it's all about sacrifice, but more than helping them pay for college, a better financial gift would be not having them have to worry about or support you in your retirement.

My children played a significant role in encouraging me to pursue FI, I am uncertain whether I would have been as driven to achieve it and leave my job if it weren't for them. As soon as I became a parent, I began to appreciate the value of spending more time with my kids and providing them with enriching life experiences and opportunities to have a memorable childhood. Instead of being solely motivated by the speed at which I could attain FI and the amount of money in my investment accounts, my focus shifted toward cherishing the moments with my children. This meant reevaluating how long it would take to reach our changing FI goals because we wanted to spend more on our lifestyle and current expenses than save and invest. You may find that your wants and needs shift if you begin to expand your family and that's when you come back to the initial plan you created and look at what a different path looks like based on your new needs and priorities. Remember, it's okay to change your mind and change courses.

LIVE YOUR FI LIFE NOW

Find something that motivates you even if it's not finance related. It can be related to a hobby you enjoy or want to get involved in.

What are the things that you want and wish to do when you reach FI and how can you start doing them now? Go back to what you said your Dream Day in Chapter 6 would look like ten years from now: what were some of the things that stood out for you? Did you say you wanted to take up a hobby like gardening or taking hikes? Whatever that hobby is that you envision doing in your FI life, find a way to do it now. Maybe it won't be on the same scale and you won't have as much time as you'd have without the obligation of the job, but can you start to take swimming lessons now, and begin to follow YouTube accounts that talk about gardening or whatever it is you're interested in?

When I began to take the steps I said I did in pursuit of FI, I started to realize the extent of freedom I already possessed in my present life. When I think about being completely FI, I see myself going to the gym and running/taking more walks outside and taking vacations. I started to prioritize my day to go to the gym more and take runs, and when I had the opportunity to go away with friend or to visit family, I'd make it a priority in my schedule. Sometimes that means being able to do less work for my business because I chose to go for a run instead, but it motivates me to create a balanced approach with my time and how I set goals for myself.

DON'T PUT YOUR JOY AND FREEDOM ON LAYAWAY

Too many people only look toward a vacation or their next enjoyment months or years away. It's like they've put their joy and freedom on layaway. It's not something they feel they can experience just yet because their current circumstances are not ideal. Maybe you don't live in your dream home, your commute sucks, your job and the people you work with irritate you. So living in the next is how you get through the day. But the mindset of constantly looking forward to your next home, or next job, or having more money often creates the belief that true enjoyment of life will only begin once those milestones are achieved. The thing about living too much in the future or waiting for the next is that by the time you accomplish or have those things, your life has passed you by. Even worse, you realize that getting to the next thing doesn't solve the deeper problems or unsatisfied feelings you carried with you. This is why figuring out how to enjoy the now no matter where you are is critical to a peaceful and sustainable journey. If you can remove money or the lack of money as a barrier to your everyday happiness and find more joy right from where you are while still pursuing your goals and dreams, you've successfully cracked the code.

While writing this book, I wanted to be able to go on a writing retreat and be able to wake up to the beach and listen to the waves as I wrote while taking dips in the water and sipping on a cocktail. I thought I had to be somewhere else or be someone else to make that happen. Then I remembered that there was a beach fifteen minutes from where I lived and while it was no blue water, white sands of the Caribbean, it was a beach. I could write and create from there just as I would from anywhere. So instead of waiting or longing to make my pristine vision a reality, I chose to turn my current reality into the dream I wanted for myself. When I close my eyes the water hitting the shoreline sounds and feels the same at NYC's Rockaway Beach as it does the beaches of Jamaica.

Sure, there are a lot of differences too and if I had my pick I'd pick the blue waters of the Caribbean beaches every time without question, but what I have and what I will enjoy because it's more accessible (and free) are the beaches of NYC. Why wait for the few times a year that I can make it to an island beach when I can enjoy the beach fifteen minutes away?

Making the best of what you have and enjoying what is available to you is not lowering your standards or a sign that you've given up on your dreams. You can still want more and other things, but there is power in knowing wherever you are or what you have, you can make the best of it.

Continue to Follow the STEPs

STEP stands for Support, Tools, Education, and Plan. In order to stay persistent and consistent on your FI journey, you'll need to have and continue the following:

Support: We talked a lot about how important community is for a happy and successful FI journey. Find your community and support system, whether online or in person, to help keep you motivated to reach your goals.

Tools: Find the right tools to help you manage your money and track your progress toward your goals. This can look like budgeting apps, bank apps, and worksheets to help you manage and track your money and progress.

Education: Continue to educate yourself around money and self-development topics. Read books, take relevant courses, and listen to podcasts to help you understand your options and concepts so that you can make more informed decisions.

Plan: Develop your FI plan and come back to it and adjust accordingly as your goals evolve or circumstances change.

> Get the most updated version of these resources and other tools via your complimentary Your Journey to Financial Freedom Toolkit at www.yourjourneytofinancialfreedom.com.

Part 4: Staying The Course & Enjoying the Journey Checklist

☐   Be Prepared To Change Your Mind & Plan as Necessary

☐   Find Community To Support You

☐   Get on The Same Page w/ Your Partner

☐   Consider Children, Other Dependents or Responsibilities

☐   Celebrate Your Wins (Big & Small)

☐   Continue the STEPs (Support, Tools, Education & Plan)

☐   Enjoy The Journey

CONCLUSION

The hero's journey is a common storytelling template. The main character—the hero—goes on an adventure, faces various challenges, and undergoes a transformation. The hero's journey concept was popularized by Joseph Campbell in his book *The Hero with a Thousand Faces*, where he separated the hero's journey into distinct stages. The beginning stage of every hero's journey is the call, when the hero receives information or something happens that compels the hero to go off on an adventure. The hero can decide to either answer or refuse the call. While the hero will experience challenges and setbacks, the reward for going on the journey far outweighs any struggle they encounter. In the end, the hero accomplishes their mission and returns to their normal world or life equipped with knowledge, and maybe even a greater sense of confidence and freedom.

You are the hero in your life's story and in the story of your financial journey. The inner call you heard that made you pick up this book or told you that there is something else out there for you was not by mistake.

While the journey to reach complete financial independence is a daring and bold pursuit, you now know too much to ignore the call. Just because this pursuit seems insurmountable at times doesn't mean it's impossible for you to achieve a different and improved version of your current life. You don't need to have $1 million in your investment accounts or have your student debt completely paid off to feel good and proud of yourself and the progress you'll make. You don't need to give up having fun or spending money on vacations or whatever truly makes you happy in order to achieve your version of financial freedom and independence. There is a way to find balance.

It was only a few years ago that I felt stuck in a job and didn't see how I could break free from the corporate golden handcuffs. When I discovered financial independence, I heard the call. With more knowledge came inspiration to take action and finally answer the call. With more action, I saw more possibilities and opportunities. My life today looks completely different than it did when I was stuck in that commute and cubicle. My circumstances didn't change overnight, but I felt compelled to take the pathway that slowly unfolded before me.

The life you desire is waiting for you too. Success is achievable as long as you never permanently give up and are willing to make the necessary changes for the results you want. Recognizing the importance of implementing practical steps and strategies is essential. However, equally important is acknowledging the significance of the intangible and internal work that must be done: the process of self-reflection and personal growth. To succeed, you'll need to know how to increase your income, optimize your expenses, pay off debt, and invest, but you'll also need to know how to improve your mindset and habits. I want you to reach inner wealth before you obtain the external wealth—to be at peace and find happiness regardless of your financial situation.

As you move forward and begin to take action, remember that some of the changes you make will be incremental. They may feel insignificant in the moment, but they are the actions that will allow you to reap significant results. Actions like finally starting (and trying to stick to) that budget, reaching out to a colleague to talk to them about a job you want to apply for, or taking twenty minutes to read up on a financial concept that feels foreign to you all add up over time. Don't be discouraged if you don't immediately see all the outcomes you want. The changes are happening, even if you can't see the results right away in your bank account.

This book is meant to be a guide and a reference for you to come back to as many times as you need. By implementing even one of the strategies, or by reframing the way you look at your finances through the lens of a concept presented in this book, you can change your life. With perseverance and a willingness to learn and adapt, financial independence is within your reach.

I love to hear from fellow Journeyers so please connect with me. Let me know your biggest takeaways and aha moments. I'm JourneyToLaunch/@JourneyToLaunch on every social media platform. Go to www.journeytolaunch.com and listen to the *Journey to Launch* podcast to continue this journey with me.

XO
Jamila

ACKNOWLEDGMENTS

To my amazing mom, Debby. Thank you for allowing me to grow without limits. Your love and support make me feel like I can do and be anything. Your hard work and sacrifice truly shaped me into the woman I am today. There aren't enough words to say how much I love you.

Zach, Luke and Blake—you push and teach me in ways that I didn't know were possible. Zach, when I was pregnant with you on that long commute, you made me want more for my life and our future family. Luke, you inspired me to put my ideas out into the world. Blake, once I found out that I was pregnant with you, I knew I had to go for it and give it my all. You three gave me the courage to follow my dreams.

Woody, when we met as freshmen in college, we were so young and just learning about the real world. We've built such an extraordinary life together over the last twenty-plus years. Thank you for always supporting me and being down for whatever. I couldn't have written this book without your support and love.

To my siblings, Sam, Shani, Imani, Zadeki, Nzingha, Shaina, and Sonya—I love you and cherish our bond. Thank you, Shaina, for going into super-aunty mode and helping with the kids after school while I tried to meet my writing deadlines in the midst of sneaking in my naps and walks outside.

Shaleia, you've been by my side since we were fourteen. Your loyalty and love have been unmatched—thank you for always having my back. Dorianne, I want to express my gratitude for your unwavering support and friendship. Your presence in my life has been invaluable. Tiffany, thank you for your sisterhood and love.

To Sis, Aunt Lin, Polly, Aunt Joanie, Aunt Jackie, Gramps, Mumma, Aunt Sheryl, Mummy, and Poppy, my Souffrant family and all my aunties, uncles, cousins and friends—thank you for showing me the value of family and community. It's powerful to know that I have you in my corner rooting for me. I love you all dearly.

Meghan, thank you for your work in articulating my scattered thoughts into an incredible book proposal. To my amazing book agents, Jan and Steve, thanks for helping me to get the best possible book deal as a first-time author. To Amanda, my book coach, thank you for calming my fears, fixing my run-on sentences and being one of my biggest cheerleaders in this process. Thank you to my editor, Peter Joseph, and the wonderful team at Hanover Square Press and HarperCollins, who have been involved in every step of this book's journey from first draft to its release into the world.

Johanna, as my right hand in all things *Journey to Launch*, I appreciate you and all that you do behind the scenes. Vee, Kayli, and Ava—thank you for your help in getting my work out into the world. Emily, thank you for making me sound smart with your podcast editing magic. To Adam, my agent, thank you for fighting for every dollar and for advocating on my behalf.

Thank you to all the *Journey to Launch* podcast guests who have generously shared their stories and expertise. I also want to express my appreciation to my fellow creators, many of whom have become friends and inspirations.

To my home island of Jamaica and fellow Jamaicans—I may have left as a baby but you're always in my heart. To the city that raised me, NYC, and specifically the borough of Brooklyn, I hope I'm making you proud.

Lastly, I want to express my gratitude to my fellow Journeyers, who have been with me since the early days of my podcast, listening to every episode from the start, as well as to those who have just discovered me. Every time you left an encouraging comment or shared a kind word about my work, it encouraged me to keep going. I wouldn't be here doing what I love without you. Thank you!

APPENDIX

FINANCIAL GOALS—PRIORITIZE

STEP 1: Write out all your goals (financial or lifestyle) here. Don't worry about prioritizing them, just "dump" them all out below.

STEP 2: Next to each goal write F for financial goal and L for lifestyle goal.

STEP 3: Next to each financial goal write if it's an Income, Spending, Saving, Investing or Debt Payoff goal.

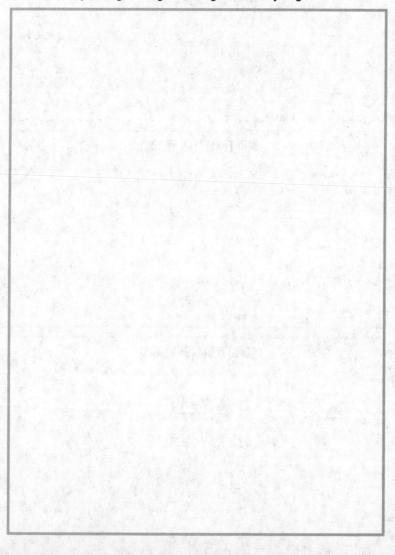

FINANCIAL GOALS—PRIORITIZE

STEP 4: Break out your goals in the 3 time frame categories below.

SHORT OR IMMEDIATE (WITHIN 1 YEAR):

MID TERM (1–5 YEARS):

LONG TERM (5+ YEARS):

FINANCIAL GOALS—PRIORITIZE

STEP 5: Take the top 5 goals from each category on the previous page and prioritize them in order of importance. What would you like to accomplish first?

SHORT OR IMMEDIATE (WITHIN 1 YEAR):

1.

2.

3.

4.

5.

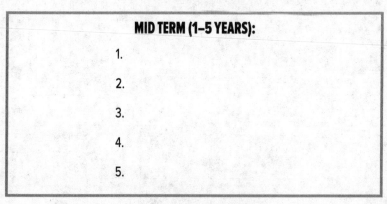

MID TERM (1–5 YEARS):

1.

2.

3.

4.

5.

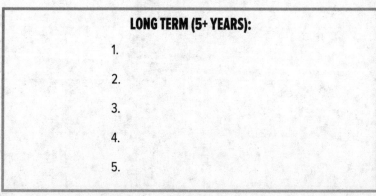

LONG TERM (5+ YEARS):

1.

2.

3.

4.

5.

FINANCIAL AND LIFESTYLE GOALS— GOAL PLANNER

Figure out how much is needed to
accomplish or experience your goal.

GOAL	TIME NEEDED	AMOUNT NEEDED	SAVINGS PER MONTH
Example: Down payment for home	5 years (60 months)	$20,000	$333 ($20,000 ÷ 60)

SELF PERFORMANCE ASSESSMENT AND CHALLENGE WORKSHEET

Current Salary _____   Salary Goal _____

CURRENT SELF PERFORMANCE ASSESSMENT

☐ Okay   ☐ Average   ☐ Good   ☐ Great   ☐ Exceptional

How can you improve your performance at your job?
What actionable things can you do starting today?

TWO-WEEK CHALLENGE

Write down five things you will do differently; stretch yourself for the day.
At the end of the day, compare them to what was actually accomplished.

WEEK ONE:

WEEK TWO:

WEEK THREE:

WEEK FOUR:

WEEK FIVE:

DEBT ASSESSMENT WORKSHEET

You can choose to list your debts by highest interest rate to lower interest rate
or lowest balance depending on how you intend to pay off your debt

NON-MORTGAGE DEBTS

List all your debts not including mortgage
(credit cards, student loans, personal loans, car loans, etc.)

Creditor	Total Remaining Balance Owed	Interest Rate	Minimum Monthly Payment
	$	%	$
	$	%	$
	$	%	$
	$	%	$
	$	%	$
	$	%	$
	$	%	$
	$	%	$
	$	%	$
	$	%	$
	$	%	$
	$	%	$
TOTAL:	$		$

STUDENT LOAN DEBTS

List your student loan debt

Issuer	Total Remaining Balance Owed	Interest Rate	Minimum Monthly Payment
	$	%	$
	$	%	$
	$	%	$
TOTAL:	$		$

MORTGAGE DEBTS

List your mortgage debt
(primary property and investment properties)

Primary or Investment	Total Remaining Balance Owed	Interest Rate	Minimum Monthly Payment
	$	%	$
	$	%	$
	$	%	$
TOTAL:	$		$

TOTAL DEBTS:	$

PODCAST EPISODES MENTIONED

1. Purple—Episode 126: How She's Building A $500,000 Portfolio & Retiring Early At 30 Years Old & Episode 289: *Retiring at 30yrs Old & Living A Full Life On $20k A Year W/ Purple* (pg 34–35 & pg 125) journeytolaunch. com/episode126 & journeytolaunch.com/episode289

2. Veronique—Episode 109: *From Living Paycheck to Paycheck to Paying Off Debt & Financially Thriving* (pg 52–53) journeytolaunch.com/episode109

3. Cassandra—Episode 111: *How Cassandra Increased Her Income by $10k & Improved Her Money Mindset* (pg 66–67) journeytolaunch.com/episode111

4. Jon Acuff—Episode 236: *How To Change Overthinking From A Super Problem To A Superpower* (pg 85–86) journeytolaunch.com/episode236

5. Ariana—Episode 294: *How Ariana Paid Off $68K of Credit Card Debt, Quit Her Job & Found A Budgeting System That Worked* (pg 154–155 & pg 230) journeytolaunch.com/episode294

6. Josie—Episode 113: *Life After Becoming Debt Free* (pg 198) journeytolaunch.com/episode113

7. Tracy—Episode 296: *How Tracy Paid Off $170K Of Debt, Why We Need More Queer Voices In The FIRE Movement & Being Open About Privilege* (pg 210–211) journeytolaunch.com/episode296

8. Norly—Episode 278: *How Norly Jean-Charles Found Financial Independence, Saved Half Her Income & Bought Her Mom A Home* (pg 225) journeytolaunch.com/episode278

9. Tasha—Episode 243: *From Side Hustle To Million Dollar Virtual Assistant Business With Tasha Booth* (pg 231) journeytolaunch.com/episode243

10. Leilani—Episode 270: *Retiring Early, Paying Off The Mortgage, & Having Space To Focus On Joy* (pg 291–292) journeytolaunch.com/episode270

11. Ledo & Shameka—Episode 139: *Love & Money: How They Got On The Same Page To Pay Off $32,000 of Debt w/ LeDo & Shameka McDowell* (pg 311) journeytolaunch.com/episode139

To listen to all the *Journey to* Launch podcast episodes, go to *journeytolaunch.com* or listen on your favorite podcast app.

Your Journey to Financial Freedom Complete Checklist

Part 1: The What, Why & How of Financial Independence

- [ ] Understand The Concepts of Financial Independence and Financial Freedom

- [ ] Discover Your Current Journeyer Stage

- [ ] Know the 4 Tangible Components of the FI Formula

- [ ] Know the 2 Intangible Components of the FI Formula

Part 2: Creating Your Enjoyable Financial Independence Plan

- [ ] Assess Your Current Mindset & Habits

- [ ] Uncover The Desired Guac Level You Want To Live Now & in FI

- [ ] Identify Your Lifestyle Goals

- [ ] Organize & Prioritize Your Financial Goals

- [ ] Know Your Current Numbers (Income, Expenses, Assets & Liabilities)

- [ ] Forecast Your Future Numbers (FI #, Income, Expenses, Assets & Liabilities)

- [ ] Create A Budget That Includes Your Financial Goals & Life-style Goals

☐   Map Out Different Scenarios of How Long It Will Take You To Reach Your FI Goals

Part 3: Executing Your Financial Independence Plan
Step 1: Optimize Expenses

☐   Evaluate Your Expenses

☐   Identify Expenses To Eliminate & Reduce

☐   Identify Expenses To Increase

☐   Improve Mindset & Habits Around Expenses

☐   Take Action on Optimizing Expenses

☐   Call Service Providers & Negotiate Rates

☐   Downsize or Eliminate Costly Expenses if Possible

☐   Eliminate or Reduce Daily or Recurring Expenses

☐   Spend More in Areas That Bring You Joy or Are Helpful

☐   Put Money Saved From Optimizing Expenses Towards Financial & Lifestyle Goals

Step 2: Increase Income

☐   Evaluate Your Income

☐   Identify Ways To Increase Your Income Through Current Job

☐   Identify Ways To Increase Your Income Through Other Job/Careers

☐   Identify Ways To Increase Your Income Through Side Hustles & Entrepreneurship

- [ ] Improve Mindset & Habits Around Income

- [ ] Take Action on Increasing Income

- [ ] Negotiate Salary at Current Job

- [ ] Interview At Other Jobs & Negotiate New Salary

- [ ] Execute Side Hustle & Entrepreneurship Ideas

- [ ] Put Additional Money Earned From Increasing Income Towards Financial & Lifestyle Goals

Step 3: Pay Down Liabilities/Debt
- [ ] Evaluate Your Liabilities

- [ ] Create A Debt Payoff Plan

- [ ] Improve Mindset & Habits Around Debt

- [ ] Take Action on Decreasing Debt

- [ ] Include Debt Payoff Plan in Budget

- [ ] Set up Automatic Debt Payments

- [ ] Increase Debt Payments When Possible

Step 4: Increase Assets
- [ ] Evaluate Your Assets

- [ ] Identify Savings Goals

- [ ] Identify Investing Goals

☐ Create a Saving & Investing Plan

☐ Improve Mindset & Habits Around Increasing Assets

☐ Take Action on Increasing Assets

☐ Include Saving & Investing Goals in Budget

☐ Open up High-Yield Savings Account

☐ Invest up to Company Match for 401(K)

☐ Open Roth IRA

☐ Open Taxable Account

☐ Increase Contributions to Pre-Tax Retirement Accounts & Taxable Accounts

☐ Set Up Automatic Contributions to Investment Accounts

Part 4: Staying The Course & Enjoying The Journey
☐ Be Prepared To Change Your Mind & Plan as Necessary

☐ Find Community To Support You

☐ Get on The Same Page w/ Your Partner

☐ Consider Children, Other Dependents or Responsibilities

☐ Celebrate Your Wins (Big & Small)

☐ Continue the STEPs (Support, Tools, Education & Plan)

☐ Enjoy The Journey

REFERENCES

Chapter 1

"standard retirement age (between sixty-five and sixty-seven years old)..." *https://www.ssa.gov/oact/progdata/nra.html*

"49% of adults ages fifty-five to sixty-sixy who had no personal retirement savings in 2017." *https://www.census.gov/library/stories/2022/01/women-more-likely-than-men-to-have-no-retirement-savings.html*

Chapter 5

"They take no effort to think and are the..." *Soundtracks: The Surprising Solution to Overthinking* by Jon Acuff, Baker Books, 2021, pp. 22, 27

Chapter 6

"George Kinder, a financial planner, author, and founder..." *https://www.kinderinstitute.com/*

"This is due to what psychologists refer to as prospection..." *https://en.m.wikipedia.org/wiki/Prospection*

"...the greater connection you feel between who you are today, your nearer self..." *https://greatergood.berkeley.edu/article/item/how_thinking_ about_the_future_makes_life_more_meaningful*

Chapter 8

"The 4% Rule is attributed to Bill Bengen..." *https://www.investopedia. com/terms/f/four-percent-rule.asp*

Chapter 9

"Americans spend an average of $1,497 per month or $18,000 a year on nonessential items..." *https://swnsdigital.com/us/2019/05/ americans-spend-at-least-18000-a-year-on-these-non-essential-costs/*

"It reminds me of a story by motivational speaker and author Les Brown..." From "Dog On a Nail" analogy in Ultimate Guide to Success: The Power of Purpose; The Greatness Within You; The Courage to Live Your Dreams *https://www.google.com/books/edition/Les_Brown_ Ultimate_Guide_to_Success/NHh3EAAAQBAJ?hl=en&gbpv=0*

"Researchers studied data collected from 1986 to 2002..." *https:// knowledge.wharton.upenn.edu/podcast/knowledge-at-wharton-podcast/ conspicuous-consumption-and-race-who-spends-more-on-what/* More up-dated resources at: *https://www.bls.gov/cex/csxann02.pdf* and *https:// www.bls.gov/cex/tables/calendar-year/mean-item-share-average-standard-error/reference-person-race-2021.pdf*

"...the Pew Research Center's 2020 study which found that..." *https:// www.brookings.edu/blog/up-front/2020/12/08/the-black-white-wealth-gap-left-black-households-more-vulnerable/ https://www.federalreserve. gov/econres/notes/feds-notes/disparities-in-wealth-by-race-and-ethnicity-in-the-2019-survey-of-consumer-finances-20200928.html*

Chapter 10

"Many high earners are only income rich and not balance sheet rich..." *https://money.usnews.com/money/personal-finance/family-finance/articles/ where-do-i-fall-in-the-american-economic-class-system*

"The federal poverty threshold for a single person in 2022..." *https:// www.healthcare.gov/glossary/federal-poverty-level-fpl/*

"As of 2021, the US Census Bureau reports that..." *https://www.census. gov/content/dam/Census/library/visualizations/2022/demo/p60-276/ figure2.pdf*

Chapter 11

"According to recent data from the Federal Reserve..." *https://www. newyorkfed.org/microeconomics/hhdc*

"For marginalized people and people of color..." *https://www.brookings. edu/blog/up-front/2020/12/08/the-black-white-wealth-gap-left-black-households-more-vulnerable/*

"The wealth gap in the US for Black individuals is significant, as high-lighted by the Pew Research Center's 2020 study, which found that Black households have a median net worth." *https://www.brook-ings.edu/articles/the-black-white-wealth-gap-left-black-households-more-vulnerable/*

Chapter 12

"Conversely, defined contribution plans were more prevalent for pri-vate industry workers..." *https://www.bls.gov/opub/btn/volume-12/ how-do-retirement-plans-for-private-industry-and-state-and-local-government-workers-compare.htm*

"Over time, since its inception in 1928..." *https://www.officialdata.org/us/ stocks/s-p-500/1928?amount=100&endYear=2022*

"On average, index funds have a management..." *https://www.ici.org/ system/files/2022-03/per28-02_2.pdf*

"Unless your actively managed fund outperforms the passively man-aged index fund..." *https://www.spglobal.com/spdji/en/documents/spiva/ spiva-us-year-end-2021.pdf*

INDEX